DORAH SITOLE
and True Love Magazine

COOKING FROM
CAPE to
CAIRO

INTRODUCTION

It has always been my wish to document the culinary experiences of my continent, Africa. What seemed to be an insurmountable task or a dream, happened sooner than I had anticipated.

IN ZULU WE SAY: *'Ukwanda kwaliwa umthakathi'* (only a witch will stand in the way of progress). This cookbook had to happen and only a magazine like True Love, that recognizes the virtues of Africa and its people, could put it together.

It would give me great joy to see African food, in its entirety, on the centre stage of the worlds' cuisine. The few books written about African food, concentrate on West and North African cuisine. If anything is mentioned about South African cuisine, it is usually only about Afrikaans or cape Malay food. Nothing wrong with that, but there is much more – South Africa has an array of exciting local foods, from villages and vibrant townships, through to the cities. What a pleasure it was to visit all these remote corners of our beautiful land and to get to grips with our wonderful food!

My wish is that this book will continue to inspire everyone who reads it to become excited about Africa. Our cuisine is definitely the cuisine to embrace. The food that has nourished our people for centuries, is an integral part of our lives. Granted, culture is not static, but we cannot allow the basic flavours that shaped our palates to be eradicated.

North Africa with its rich Arab-influenced cuisine, has undoubtedly made an impact on international food trends. West African foods influences are seen as far as the USA, where Creole and Cajun gumbos celebrate the versatility of African ingredients. East Africa's coconuts and the wonderful spices of Zanzibar have added an exotic touch to the gourmet foods of the world. The lakes of Central Africa are teeming with fish, an important source of income and a major part of the diet. The shores of this great continent also abound with a rich variety of seafood, so fish and seafood form an important part of African cuisine.

OOKING FROM
CAPE TO
CAIRO

DORAH SITOLE

TRUE LOVE

Through the pages of this book, Southern Africa will at last make its contribution to International cuisine. Its rich, nutritious and robust foods include dry beans, samp, maize-rice and maize-meal, cornrice, sorghum, groundnuts, offal, caterpillars, dried meat and vitamin-packed morogo, unusual root vegetables like amadumbe and the more exotic meats such as ostrich and zebra. These and many other foodstuffs have nurtured the people of this continent since ancient times.

The people of Africa willingly shared their culinary secrets with me. For this I am grateful. Compiling this book would have been very difficult were it not for the kind chefs, housewives and caterers who hosted my photographers and me. I wish I had gone to each and every African country, but that would have taken a lifetime. I also wish I had documented each and every recipe from the countries I visited, but that would have filled several volumes. However, the recipes in this book are the most popular and most of them are national dishes. They will definitely give you a taste of the culinary culture of our continent! Because not all the African ingredients are well known, I have included a photographic section for easy reference.

At last there is some record of food from Cape to Cairo for our children and generations to come. I know you will get excited with these dishes, your tastebuds will be challenged by the flavours of the African continent.

May Africa accept this cookbook as my humble contribution to the African Renaissance.

DORAH SITOLE

First edition, first impression 1999
Second edition, first impression 2009
  by Tafelberg
an imprint of NB Publishers
40 Heerengracht, Cape Town 8000

Publisher: Tania de Kock
Design: PETALDESIGN
Photography: Graeme Borchers
Styling: Taryne Jakobi
Food preparation: Mokgadi Itsweng
                    and Tumelo Mushi

Photographic credits:
Copyright © photography True Love Magazine except
p. 36 © SAA Great Stock!, p. 76 Gallo Images / Dook
p. 104 Gallo Images / Sarie, p. 112 Gallo Images /
Jacques Marais, p. 70 Gallo Images/ Mark Skinner
p. 28 Roger de la Harpe / Africa Imagery /
africanpictures.net, p. 20 Shane Doyle / Independent
Contributors /africanpictures.net, p. 50 Ariadne Van
Zandbergen / Africa Imagery /africanpictures.net,
p. 100 Kim Thunder / Independent Contributors /
africanpictures.net, p. 62 Karin Duthie / Illustrative
Options / African pictures.net, p. 8; 84; 134; 142 Gallo
Images / Getty Images

Reproduction by Resolution Colour Pty (Ltd),
Cape Town, RSA
Printed and bound by Tien Wah (Pte) Ltd, Singapore

ISBN-13: 978-0-624-04746-9

Accessories courtesy of Silk & Cotton Company,
wwwArt Africa, Antony Shapiro for African Divas,
Gatehouse at Mavromac, Objekt, One on One, Lucky
Fish, Imagin Nation, Country Living, Santos, Mzansi
Collection, from the Department of Trade & Industry,
Woolworths, Loads of Living, Indaba, Sandton City.

ACKNOWLEDGEMENTS:

Some South African traditional recipes are winning
entries from *True Love Magazine*'s readers'
compitition sponsored by Fedics. The following chefs
and cooks contributed recipes:
Botswana: Chef Frank Wiese, Miss Tash Sparrow and
Mrs Sebautlwang 'Madinko' Tsheko
Egypt: Chef Faisal Abu Saada, Mrs Nadia Moursi and
Mrs Jeanette Bedewi
Ghana: Chef Alex Asare and Mrs Mercy Debrah
Kenya: Chef Gift Mwasho and Mama Omodi
KwaZulu-Natal: Chef Sipho Mataba and
Mrs Joyce Mbuyaze
Lesotho: Chef Manraz Rambocous and
Mrs Olive Makenete
Malawi: Chef John Mafemula (Nkopolo Lodge) and
Chef Richard Makawa (Mount Soche Hotel)

Morocco: Chef M'hamed Harbroune and
Mrs Minah Abuane
Mozambique: Chef Orlando Lipanga and
Mrs Joseffina Lenato Simbine
Senegal: Chef Arista Mandy and The Saint Germaine
Restaurant, Gore Island
Swaziland: Chef Musa Mkhatshwa and
Chef Dave Boyjoonauth
Transkei: Chef Emmanuel Dlamini, Mrs Mpumi
Maqungo and Mrs Joyce Phoqela
Western Cape: Chef Ralph Cupido and
Mrs Cass Abrahams
Venda: Vho Masindi Mudau
Zambia: Chefs Lee Wilson, Martin Chasunkwa and
Nchongo Daka and Mrs Doreen Mwale
Zanzibar: Chef Matloub Abdul, Chef Issa Khamis
Mohamed, Mr Dipak Joshi and Miss Rabia Mwini
Zimbabwe: Chef Charles Musakaruka

CONTENTS

COOKING FROM CAPE TO CAIRO

CAPE MALAY

THE WESTERN CAPE, characterised by a succession of majestic mountain ranges, is perhaps most famous for Cape Town's Table Mountain, and the spectacular flowering plants that grace the mountain slopes and the surrounding countryside. Best known is the protea, among them the king protea, the country's floral emblem, which grows abundantly in the region.

The Cape, however, is also where many of the country's cultures meet and blend. It is here that the Muslim community, commonly referred to as the Cape Malays, has established itself. The Cape Malay people, largely descendants of slaves and exiled dissidents from the East, are a perfect blend of Africa and the East. The Dutch settlers, who arrived at the Cape in 1652, brought with them highly skilled slaves from Indonesia and Malaysia to build the prosperity of their colony. The Cape's distinctive architecture attests to the skill and craftsmanship of these people.

The Dutch encountered indigenous Khoisan people hunting, herding sheep, and gathering veldkos and seafood. It was, however, the arrival of the Muslims that had the most influence on the local cuisine. The slaves and exiles introduced a variety of spices into the dishes prepared for their Dutch masters.

They skillfully blended the ingredients and slowly exposed the mixture to moist heat while maintaining the essential goodness of each ingredient. This method of cooking has evolved over 300 years and has resulted in what is known today as Cape Malay cuisine.

The Cape Malay community has retained its love for food, and each dish is still enhanced with exotic spices. Typical and much-favoured dishes include bobotie, chicken masala, roti, denningvleis, breyani, bredies, and boeber. Bredies, or stews, and curries are usually served with yellow rice with raisins, and sambals.

MUTTON BREYANI

SERVES 6-8

1,5 kg (3½ lb) mutton on the bone
250 ml (1 cup) oil
3 large onions, sliced
15 ml (1 T) crushed ginger
15 ml (1 T) crushed garlic
6 medium potatoes, cubed
5 ml (1 t) salt
500 g (18 oz)/625 ml (2½ cups) basmati rice
250 g (9 oz)/375 ml (1½ cups) brown lentils
6 hard-boiled eggs
100 g (4 oz)/100 ml (7 T) butter, melted
3 ml (½ t) saffron

MARINADE:
3 sticks cinnamon
5 cardamom pods
2 green chillies
2 ml (½ t) turmeric
5 ml (1 t) red masala
30 ml (2 T) breyani masala
5 whole cloves
5 peppercorns
1 large tomato, diced
250 ml (1 cup) buttermilk

GARNISH:
2 ml (½ t) saffron
30 ml (2 T) coriander
2 hard-boiled eggs, halved

Wash the mutton and cut into cubes. Prepare the marinade and marinate meat for 2 hours.

Heat the oil, add the onions, ginger and garlic and sauté until brown. Add the marinated meat and cook for 30 minutes.

Season the potatoes with salt and fry until golden. Parboil the rice, then strain and rinse.

Place the lentils in hot water and cook until soft. Slice the boiled eggs in half.

Spoon rice into a large baking dish, followed by layers of potatoes, meat, eggs and lentils.

Repeat the layers, ending with a layer of rice mixed with butter and saffron. Cover with grease-proof paper and bake for 1 hour at 160 °C (325 °F/gas 3).

Garnish with saffron, coriander and eggs.

ONION SAMBAL

MAKES ± 250 ML (1 CUP)

2 large onions, sliced
60 ml (4 T) each coarse salt and
   brown vinegar
30 ml (2 T) smooth apricot jam
60 ml (4 T) chopped coriander leaves (dhania)

Place the onions in a bowl and sprinkle with
the salt.

Gently rub the salt and onion together with the
fingertips to remove all bitter onion juice.

Wash thoroughly in a sieve under cold running water
to remove the salt. Return to the bowl.

Mix the vinegar and apricot jam and pour over
the onions. Sprinkle with coriander leaves and serve
with any bredie.

CARROT AND CHILLI SAMBAL

MAKES ± 500 ML (2 CUPS)

4 carrots, peeled and grated
salt to taste
2 red chillies, chopped
2½ ml (½ t) sugar
15 ml (1 T) currants

Sprinkle a little salt over the carrots, leave for about
15 minutes and drain.

Add the remaining ingredients and chill until needed.

TOMATO BREDIE

SERVES 4-6

2 large onions, sliced
2 ml (½ t) peppercorns
2 ml (½ t) ground cloves
125 ml (½ cup) water
25 ml (2 T) vegetable oil
2 sticks cinnamon
1 kg (2½ lb) mutton, cut into cubes
30 mm (1 in) piece fresh ginger, finely
    chopped
2 cardamom pods
1 kg (2½ lb) very ripe tomatoes, chopped or 3
    tins (3 x 410 g/14 oz) chopped tomatoes
1 green chilli, chopped
6 medium potatoes, peeled and halved
salt, freshly ground pepper and
sugar to taste
chopped parsley

Place the onions, peppercorns, cloves and water in a large saucepan and heat until boiling. Simmer until all the water has been absorbed.

Add the oil and cinnamon and braise until the onions are golden. Add the meat, ginger and cardamom pods and stir thoroughly.

Turn down the heat, cover the saucepan with a tight-fitting lid and simmer for 30 minutes.

Add the tomatoes and chilli. Close the lid and simmer for 20 minutes.

Add the potatoes, salt, freshly ground pepper and sugar. Replace the lid and simmer until the potatoes are cooked.

Garnish with chopped parsley and serve on a bed of yellow rice (see page 15).

Chicken may be used instead of mutton but then the cooking time must be reduced to 60 minutes.

BOBOTIE

SERVES 8

2 thick slices stale white bread
250-300 ml (1-1½ cups) water
2 large onions, chopped
15 ml (1 T) vegetable oil
50 g (2 oz)/50 ml (3 T) butter
800 g (1½ lb) beef mince
3 garlic cloves, crushed
15 ml (1 T) masala
5 ml (1 t) turmeric
10 ml (2 t) ground cumin
10 ml (2 t) ground coriander

3 whole cloves
2 ml (½ t) peppercorns
5 allspice
125 ml (½ cup) sultanas
60 ml (4 T) flaked almonds
5 ml (1 t) dried mixed herbs
25 ml (2 T) chutney
salt and freshly ground black pepper to taste
6-8 lemon leaves
250 ml (1 cup) milk
2 eggs, beaten

Soak the bread in the water.

Fry the onions in the oil and butter until just transparent.

Place all the other ingredients, except the bread, lemon leaves, milk and eggs, in a large bowl and mix.

Add the fried onions in their oil to the mixture. Squeeze the water from the bread, add to the meat and mix well.

Spread in a greased ovenproof dish. Roll the lemon leaves into spikes and insert into the mixture.

Bake at 180 °C (350 °F/gas 4) for 30 minutes. Lightly beat the eggs and milk together and pour over the meat. Bake until the egg mixture has set. Serve with yellow rice (see page 15).

YELLOW RICE WITH RAISINS

SERVES 6

1 litre (4 cups) water
500 ml (2 cups) uncooked
  white rice
10 ml (2 t) turmeric
2 sticks cinnamon
3 cardamom pods
salt and sugar to taste
175 ml (¾ cup) seedless raisins
  or sultanas
30 g (1 oz)/30 ml (2 T) butter

Heat the water in a saucepan until it boils. Add the rice, turmeric, cinnamon, cardamom pods, salt and sugar. Turn down the heat, cover and simmer gently for 20 minutes or until the rice is cooked through and all the liquid has been absorbed.

Pour the rice into a colander and rinse under running water to remove excess turmeric. Return to the saucepan.

Add the raisins or sultanas, mix in lightly and steam gently for a further 15 minutes.

Add the butter and fluff the rice with a fork. Serve warm with masalas or bobotie.

A lovely blend of flavours accounts for the popularity of this well-known Cape Malay dish. It used to be common practice among the Dutch and Malay communities, and to some extent still today, to serve yellow rice as part of a meal after a funeral. The method of colouring rice with turmeric was introduced by the Indian immigrants.

WATERBLOMMETJIEBREDIE

SERVES 6

125 ml (½ cup) water
500 g (18 oz) waterblommetjies, trimmed and well washed
1 potato, sliced
1 onion, sliced
1 garlic clove, crushed
salt and freshly ground black pepper to taste
5 ml (1 t) lemon juice, optional
15 ml (1 T) chopped sorrel

Let the water boil, then add the waterblommetjies, potato, onion, garlic and seasoning. Simmer for 35 minutes or until tender but still crisp.

Add the sorrel and lemon juice and heat through. Serve the stew on rice.

Waterblommetjies or Cape pondweed
(Aponogeton distachyos) grow
in the dams and vleis of the Cape.
These add body and flavour to soups
and stews. Before cooking, cut off
the stems and soak the flowers
overnight in salted water to cleanse.

DENNINGVLEIS

SERVES 8-10

3 large onions, sliced
25 ml (2 T) vegetable oil
5 plump garlic cloves, crushed
5 allspice
6 cloves
2 bay leaves
1 green chilli, finely chopped
10 ml (2 t) freshly ground black pepper
1 kg (2½ lb) mutton, cut into portions
25 ml (1 T) seedless tamarind
250 ml (1 cup) boiling water
5 ml (1 t) ground nutmeg
salt to taste

Heat the oil in a large saucepan, add the onions and fry until soft. Add the garlic, allspice, cloves, bay leaves, chilli and pepper.

Layer the meat on top of the onions. Close the saucepan with a tightly fitting lid and simmer for 30-40 minutes.

Soak the tamarind in boiling water. Allow to cool. Pour the tamarind through a sieve, pressing all the juices through with a spoon. Pour the tamarind liquid over the meat and sprinkle with nutmeg. Season to taste and simmer for 10-15 minutes. Serve with yellow rice (see page 15).

Denningvleis is a hearty meat stew flavoured with bay leaves and tamarind, creating an exciting sweet-sour flavour.

BOEBER

SERVES 4

35 g (1 oz)/45 ml (3 T) sago
125 ml (½ cup) water
50 g (2 oz)/50 ml (3 T) butter
150 g (5 oz)/250 ml (1 cup) fine vermicelli,
 broken into small pieces
8-10 cardamom pods
3 cinnamon sticks of about 25 mm (1 in) each
200 g (7 oz)/325 ml (1½ cups) sultanas
2 litres (3½ pints/8 cups) milk
400 g (14 oz)/500 ml (2 cups) sugar
a few drops of rose water to flavour (optional)

Soak the sago in the water for 30 minutes.

Melt butter in a saucepan and gently brown the vermicelli in the butter, stirring constantly to prevent it from sticking. Add the rest of the ingredients, except the rose water.

Simmer, stirring occasionally until thick and creamy. Add rose water to taste. Serve hot or cold.

VARIATION: Grated unsalted nuts and coconut may be added to vary the flavour of the boeber.

On the fifteenth night of Ramadan, the Muslim holy month, this thick, spicy milk pudding is served to celebrate the middle of the fast. More sago may be added for a thicker consistency.

THE EASTERN CAPE, traditional home of the isiXhosa people, stretches from the foot of the Drakensberg range through undulating hills and lush valleys toward the Wild Coast, and is infamous for its many tortuous roads that wind around rocky headlands and end abruptly in cliffs. The untamed wilderness of the Wild Coast boasts magnificent natural features, such as the Hole-in-the-Wall, the Waterfall Bluff and vast rocky reefs that extend far out to sea.

Traditionally, the isiXhosa lived in homesteads where the members were all related to the head of the clan. Today, most still reside in the Cape, with a greater concentration of *ezilalini* (villages) along the eastern coastal strip, in the former homelands of Transkei and Ciskei. The Eastern Cape is predominantly rural and the traditional homesteads of the isiXhosa still lay scattered over the veld here. Many remain true to their cultural heritage: women tend to the home and lands, while the menfolk earn the family's keep.

The isiXhosa are divided into a number of large clans, including the Thembu, Bomvana, Mpondo and others, and their lively native tongue is characterised by clicking sounds. Like most other African peoples, the isiXhosa traditionally wore skin garments. Later, they used blankets dyed with a particular type of red soil, hence the term 'the red blanket people'. Women wore large turbans, beads, copper bracelets and braided skirts, while a long pipe was a status symbol of a mature married woman. Many women in the rural areas still wear the traditional apparel, but in the cities these are worn only occasionally or for celebrations.

Maize – whole, dried, crushed or ground – is a staple food in most of Africa, but it is the isiXhosa who must surely be the custodians of this versatile grain. Although they contributed samp and beans to South Africa's cuisine, their influence has extended far beyond that. Their popular soup, *isopho*, is a combination of beans and corn, and *umqa* is fresh pumpkin mashed with corn. *Amarhewu*, *imbila*, *umphokoqo* – you name it, it is certain to contain some form of maize.

INYAMA YEGUSHA
Mutton Casserole

SERVES 4

60 ml (4 T) oil
1 kg (2½ lb) mutton, cut into pieces
4 medium onions, chopped
500 g (8 oz) carrots, sliced
2 large tomatoes, chopped
salt and pepper to taste
60 g (2½ oz)/125 ml (½ cup) flour

Heat the oil and brown the meat.

Add onion, carrots, tomatoes and seasoning.

Simmer gently for 45 minutes or until the meat is cooked and tender.

Mix flour and a little water to a paste and add to meat. Simmer until thickened. Serve with samp and beans (see the recipe for *umngqusho* page 25).

ULUSHU LWENKOMO
Stewed Ox Tripe

SERVES 4-6

1 kg (2½ lb) stomach
1 kg (2½ lb) intestines
water
salt and pepper to taste

Clean the stomach and intestines thoroughly. Rinse under cold running water.

Place in a saucepan and cover with salted water. Heat until boiling, reduce the heat and simmer gently for 3 hours or until very soft. Serve with pap (porridge) or dumpling.

UMQA
Pumpkin and Corn

SERVES 4

2 kg (4½ lb) pumpkin
125 ml (½ cup) water
5 ml (1 t) salt
sugar to taste
1 kg (2½ lb)/4 x 250 ml (4 cups) whole kernel
    corn, cooked and off the cob
250 ml (1 cup) water

Peel and dice the pumpkin. Place pumpkin
in a saucepan and add the water and salt.

Cook gently for about 15 minutes until the
pumpkin is soft. Add sugar.

Stir in the corn and simmer gently for
another 15 minutes. Mash and serve.

INYAMA YENKUKHU
Chicken Casserole

SERVES 4-6

1 whole chicken of 750 g-1 kg (1½ lb-2½ lb)
60 ml (4 T) oil
4 medium onions, chopped
2 large tomatoes, chopped
salt and pepper to taste
75 ml (5 T) butter
30 ml (2 T) flour
50 ml water

Cut the chicken into pieces.

Heat the oil and fry the chicken until
golden-brown. Add the onions and cook
for 5 minutes.

Add the tomatoes and seasoning, and
simmer gently for 45 minutes or until cooked.

Thicken the casserole with the flour, mixed
with a little cold water. Serve with dumpling.

This dish is traditionally made
using *umleqwa*, or chicken
slaughtered at home.

ISOPHO
Maize and Bean Soup

SERVES 4

500 ml (2 cups) fresh maize,
   cut from the cob
250 ml (1 cup) dried sugar beans,
   soaked overnight
500 ml (2 cups) water
15 ml (1 T) oil
1 onion, chopped
5 ml (1 t) curry powder
1 potato, diced
salt to taste

Cook the maize and dried beans in the
water until tender.

Heat the oil and fry the onion, curry powder
and potato.

Add the onion and potato to the maize
soup and simmer for about 1 hour, or until
cooked. Serve hot.

INKUKHU NEMBOTJI
Chicken Strips with Green Beans

SERVES 4-6

450 ml (2 cups) oil
1 onion, sliced
3 chicken breasts, deboned and cut into strips
salt to taste
5 ml (1 t) mixed masala, such as ginger and
   garlic masala
250 ml (1 cup) green beans
250 ml (1 cup) chicken stock

Heat the oil and fry the onion until golden-
brown. Add the chicken strips and continue
to fry until soft. Sprinkle with salt and spices.

Wash and trim the green beans, but keep
them whole. Add the beans and the stock to
the chicken, and simmer gently until cooked
through. Season with salt.

TO SERVE: Gently mix into cooked samp
and beans or pile on top (see the recipe for
umngqusho on page 25).

UMNGQUSHO
Samp and Beans

SERVES 4-6

600 g (1½ lb)/750 ml (3 cups) samp and beans
water
salt to taste

Soak the samp and beans overnight.

Rinse the samp and beans and place it in a saucepan. Pour in fresh water to cover, add salt and heat until boiling.

Simmer until tender, adding water whenever the samp and beans get dry. Cooking time is about 2 hours.

Samp is made from maize kernels that have been stamped and broken but not ground as fine as maize-rice or maize-meal. Ready-mixed packets of samp and sugar beans can be bought from supermarkets. If these are not available you can mix samp and sugar beans in equal quantities.

IMBILA
Sour Porridge

SERVES 4

240 g (9 oz)/500 ml (2 cups) maize-meal
120 g (4½ oz)/250 ml (1 cup) sorghum
1 litre (4 cups) water

Soak the maize-meal and sorghum overnight in the water. Retain the water.

Cook the mixture in the water in which it soaked for 20-30 minutes, stirring constantly. The porridge must be very runny; add boiling water if it thickens too much.

Allow the porridge to cool and let it rest for 4 hours so that the fermentation process can take place. Add sugar to taste before drinking.

MAIZE WITH UMFINO

SERVES 4-6

1 medium cabbage, shredded
1 bunch spinach, shredded
1 bunch turnips, peeled and diced
1 bunch spring onions, chopped
500 ml (2 cups) water
170 g (6 oz)/250 ml (1 cup) maize-rice
180 g (6 oz)/375 ml (1½ cups) maize-meal
125 g (4½ oz)/125 ml (½ cup) butter/margarine
salt and pepper to taste

Wash and rinse the vegetables.

In a large saucepan, let the water boil and then add all the vegetables. Toss with a fork to mix and simmer for 10 minutes.

Add the maize-rice, mix through and then stir in the maize-meal. Use a wooden spoon to mix the ingredients to a pulp.

Cook over a low heat for 25 minutes, stirring occasionally.

Serve with meat dishes.

MAIZE-MEAL DUMPLING WITH VEGETABLES

SERVES 4

250 ml (1 cup) each milk and water
4 eggs, beaten
1 tin (410 g/14 oz) mixed vegetables, drained
50 g (2 oz)/75 ml (5 T) sugar
240 g (9 oz)/500 ml (2 cups) cake flour
120 g (4 oz)/250 ml (1 cup) maize-meal
10 ml (2 t) baking powder
boiling water

Beat the milk, water and eggs. Add the mixed vegetables.

Sift the dry ingredients together and add to the vegetable mixture.

Mix to a smooth, soft dough. Pour into a large greased enamel dish. Place the enamel dish in a saucepan about one third full of boiling water.

Steam gently for about 1 hour or until the dumpling is cooked. Add more water to the saucepan if it dries out during cooking. Serve with meat and gravy.

INTLANZI WITH CABBAGE AND TOMATO RELISH

SERVES 4

1 whole maasbanker (intlanzi) or
  any other firm white fish
60 g (2½ oz)/125 ml (½ cup) flour
salt and pepper to taste
60 ml (4 T) oil
50 g (2 oz)/50 ml (3 T) butter/
  margarine
500 ml (2 cups) cabbage, shredded

TOMATO RELISH:
30 ml (2 T) oil
1 onion, chopped
1 medium tomato, chopped
3 ml (½ t) cayenne pepper

Gut and clean the maasbanker. Coat the fish well with seasoned flour.

Heat the oil in a frying pan. Fry the fish on both sides until nicely browned and cooked.

TOMATO RELISH: Fry the onion, tomato and cayenne pepper in a little oil in a separate pan.

Meanwhile, braise the shredded cabbage in butter/margarine until soft.

Serve the fish whole on a bed of braised cabbage, samp and beans (see the recipe for umngqusho on page 25). Top with the tomato relish.

KWAZULU-NATAL IS THE TRADITIONAL HOME OF THE ZULU NATION, the largest ethnic group in South Africa. The province itself is characterised by rolling hills that stretch out to the mighty *izintaba zokhahlamba* – the Drakensberg, or Barrier of Spears – and includes outstanding inland and marine nature reserves.

The origins of the Zulu nation can be traced to the late 1600s – since then the realm has had 15 rulers, including the present Zulu king, Zwelthini. Perhaps the best known of the warrior kings is Shaka, who set out to make the Zulu nation the most powerful and most feared on the southern African subcontinent. Like all of South Africaís tribes, the majority of Zulu have become urbanised, but traditional customs are still upheld in the rural areas.

Zulu cuisine is simple, and the women must be creative with the limited selection: maize-meal, sorghum, sweet potatoes, potatoes, *amadumbe* (similar to sweet potato, but with a coarse skin), melons and pumpkin are most common ingredients. *Phutu* (crumbled porridge) is served with *amasi* (curdled milk) or tomato relish. Maize is often boiled or roasted on the cob, and women are often seen on sidewalks roasting corn on braziers and selling it to passers-by. Zulu men's favourite food is *inyama eyosiwe*, meat grilled over an open fire until it is cooked through and tender. This is served with *pap* (porridge) or samp, and is followed by a sip of sorghum beer, *umqombothi*.

The cultural heritage of KwaZulu-Natal also includes the legacy of settlers from India, whose descendants have become part of the essence of the region. Today, their legacy lives on not only in the Indian communities concentrated largely in and around Pietermaritzburg and Durban, but also in the contribution they have made to local cuisine – the exotic tastes, flavours and aroma of Eastern delights for which the cities – and, indeed, the province – is so well known.

RABBIT STEW WITH VEGETABLES

SERVES 6

1 rabbit of approximately 1,5 kg (3½ lb)
30 ml (2 T) cooking oil
1 onion, chopped
3 potatoes, quartered
3 carrots, sliced
250 ml (1 cup) sliced green beans
250 ml (1 cup) water
salt and pepper

Cut the rabbit into portions. Heat the oil in a large pot and brown the rabbit pieces.

Add the onion to the pot and fry with the rabbit pieces until the onion is brown. Layer the potatoes, carrots and green beans on the meat. Add the water and seasoning.

Cover and simmer over a low heat for 1-2 hours until the meat is tender. Serve with beetroot and leaf stew and *phutu*.

PHUTU

SERVES 4-6

250 ml (1 cup) water
360 g (12 oz)/750 ml (3 cups) maize-meal

Bring the water to the boil. Add maize-meal all at once without stirring, reduce heat and simmer about 20 minutes until cooked through.

Stir with a large fork until crumbly.

UMBIDO
Beetroot Leaf Stew

SERVES 4-6

30 ml (2 T) oil
1 onion, finely chopped
500 g (18 oz) beetroot leaves
3 tomatoes, peeled and diced
salt and pepper
4 hard-boiled eggs, chopped

Heat the oil, add the onions and fry gently until transparent.

Add the beetroot leaves, tomatoes and seasoning. Simmer gently for 10 minutes until soft. Stir occasionally with a fork.

Carefully mix in the hard-boiled eggs.

Serve on *phutu*.

THREE-LEGGED POTS
The traditional three-legged cast-iron pot has been in use since the Dark Ages. It is thought that it was introduced into Africa through European traders. Today it is used all over the world. In South Africa it has become a traditional way of cooking for most feasts or celebrations. Cooking over an open fire adds a unique flavour to the food. An added bonus is that the pot retains an even heat, which ensures that the food cooks slowly, at the same time conserving energy.

IPHALISHI LOBHONTSHISI
Butter Bean Porridge

SERVES 4

400 g (14 oz)/500 ml (2 cups) butter beans
water
salt and pepper to taste
60ml (4 T) oil
1 onion, grated
2 garlic cloves, crushed
2 tomatoes, chopped
2 beef stock cubes, dissolved in 650 ml (2½ cups) water
240 g (9 oz)/500 ml (2 cups) maize-meal

Cover the beans with water and soak overnight. Retain the water.

Bring beans and water to the boil. Season and cook until soft, then mash to a smooth paste.

Fry the onion and garlic in oil until soft. Add the tomatoes, bean paste and stock. Heat until boiling, add the maize-meal and mix well.

Cook for 35 minutes over medium heat, stirring occasionally. Serve hot with any relish.

IMPHALISHI ELIMUNCU
Sour Milk Porridge

SERVES 4

500 ml (2 cups) sour milk
water
120 g (4½ oz)/250 ml (1 cup) maize-meal
125ml (½ cup) water

Boil the sour milk and water. Add maize-meal, stir and cook for 30-35 minutes.

Serve hot with tomato and onion relish.

ISIJEZA
Pumpkin Porridge

SERVES 4

10 pumpkin slices, peeled
salt and sugar or cinnamon sugar to taste
250 ml (1 cup) cold water
500 ml (2 cups) hot water
120g (4½ oz)/250 ml (1 cup) maize-meal

Chop the pumpkin slices into small pieces. Sprinkle with salt and sugar. Add the cold water and cook until soft.

Mash the pumpkin and add the hot water. Let it boil and then add the maize-meal. Stir until well mixed.

Cook for 30 minutes over medium heat. Serve hot or cold with any relish.

UMHLUZI WETAMATISI NE ANYANISI
Tomato and Onion Relish

SERVES 4

45 ml (3 T) oil
3 onions, finely chopped
2 garlic cloves, crushed
6 large tomatoes, peeled and grated
5 ml (1 t) cayenne pepper
2 green or red chillies, seeded and chopped
salt and pepper to taste

Heat the oil, add the onions and garlic and sauté until transparent.

Add the tomatoes and all the remaining ingredients and cook through until the mixture has thickened. Serve over *phutu*.

STIR-FRIED VEGETABLES WITH SWEET POTATO CRISPS

SERVES 2

45 g (1½ oz)/45 ml (3 T) butter
2-3 leeks, cut into long strips
1 large onion, sliced
½ cabbage, finely shredded
250 g (9 oz) spinach, washed and chopped
50 g (2 oz)/125 ml (½ cup) sunflower seeds
salt and pepper to taste

CRISPS:
3 sweet potatoes, peeled and thinly sliced
750 ml (3 cups) oil
5 ml (1 t) cumin
10 ml (2 t) sea salt

Melt the butter, add the leeks, onion and cabbage. Cook until the vegetables are soft.

Add the spinach and sunflower seeds, stir to coat with butter. Season to taste.

CRISPS: Heat the oil, add the sweet potatoes and fry until golden. Drain on brown paper or paper towels. Lightly sprinkle the sweet potatoes with cumin and sea salt. Serve the vegetables in the middle of a large platter and arrange the crisps around it.

SAMP PAELLA

SERVES 2

100 g (4 oz)/ 125 ml (½ cup) samp
1 litre water
45 g (1½ oz) 45 ml (3 T) butter
1 onion, chopped
4 mushrooms, finely chopped
1 green pepper, diced
125 ml (½ cup) white wine
3 mussels
45 ml (3 T) oil
6 prawns, peeled and cleaned
100 g (4 oz) kingklip, diced
4-6 cherry tomatoes

Cook samp in water until soft – do not stir, as stirring will make it mushy. Rinse and set aside.

Melt butter, add onion and mushrooms and sauté. Add the green pepper and sauté until soft.

In a separate saucepan, heat the wine until it boils, then add the mussels. Simmer for 1 minute.

Heat the oil, add prawns and kingklip and fry.

Add the onion mixture to the fish. Add the samp, stir lightly and add the tomatoes. Spoon on a serving plate and top with the mussels.

VARIATION: Set mussels, tomatoes and prawns aside. Place samp in a mould and leave 15 minutes. Turn out on a heated serving and garnish with the mussels, tomatoes and prawns.

MAIZE-MEAL CUSTARD WITH CHOCOLATE SAUCE

SERVES 5

500 ml (2 cups) cream
10 ml (2 t) cinnamon
62,5 ml (¼ cup) sugar
3 ml (½ t) vanilla essence
180 g (6 oz)/375 ml (1½ cups)
  maize-meal
250 ml (1 cup) milk
5 prunes, stoned

TOPPING:
200 g (7 oz) dark chocolate
200 ml (1 cup) cream

Heat the cream, cinnamon, sugar and vanilla essence together.

Mix the maize-meal with the milk and add to the warm cream. Cook until thickened.

Place the prunes in the base of a mould and pour maize-meal mixture on top. Cool to set.

TOPPING: Mix the chocolate and cream, and melt in a double boiler. Turn mould out on a serving platter and pour sauce over just before serving.

FROM TIME IMMEMORIAL THE IMAGE OF LESOTHO IS THE SMOKE SEEPING THROUGH THE THATCH ROOFS OF VILLAGE HUTS, the smell of cowdung fires, early morning sunlight bathing herdboys as they scatter across the hills, the clattering hooves of horses, and the greetings of blanket-clad men: *'Khotso, pula nala'* ('Peace, rain and plenty').

Three quarters of Lesotho is dominated by the rugged and scantily populated Maluti mountains. Most of its 1,5 million population live in the lowland areas and only a small percentage live in and around the capital, Maseru. The country is completely surrounded by South Africa, and its economy and politics is thus much influenced by its larger neighbour.

The Basotho nation was created in the 19th century through the leadership of the dynamic military and diplomatic strategist, Moshoeshoe I, who forged together small chiefdoms. Basotholand merged with the Cape Colony until it was finally recognised as an independent kingdom in 1966. Today, the

Basotho people are led by King Letsie III, a direct descendant of Moshoeshoe.

Rural folk still tend to wear the colourful and symbolically patterned blankets for which they are so well known, and the men don conical hats of straw, while the women are expert weavers.

The Basotho style of cooking is basic but nutritious. The family eats only home-grown vegetables and hand-raised chicken, and anything left over from the harvest is sun dried to make *mangaganjane*. A nutritious meal could consist of *pap* (maize-meal porridge), steamed pumpkin with cinnamon, spinach stewed in beef stock, and stewed oxtail, a Basotho favourite. Beetroot salad is very popular, and a meal may be considered incomplete without it. The beetroot is cooked, grated and then mixed with chopped onion, sugar and vinegar.

SEBETE SE HALIKILOENG WITH MOROGO

Fried Liver with Morogo

SERVES 4

MOROGO:
500 g (18 oz) dry morogo (thepe)
30 ml (2 T) water
salt and pepper
90 ml (6 T) milk
30 g (1 oz)/30 ml (2 T) butter/margarine

LIVER:
500 g (18 oz) liver, cut into pieces
60 ml (4 T) oil

MOROGO: Wash the vegetables thoroughly, rinse and place in a saucepan. Add the water, salt and pepper. Cover and cook until the liquid is reduced. Add the milk and butter or margarine. Simmer until all the liquid has been absorbed.

LIVER: Prick the liver with a fork and sprinkle it with salt. Fry in hot oil on both sides for approximately 10–15 minutes.

Place the liver on the morogo. Serve with sour porridge.

TING
Sour Porridge

SERVES 4

120 g (4½ oz)/250 ml (1 cup) maize-meal
250 ml (1 cup) maize-rice
375 ml (1½ cups) water

Mix all the ingredients in a plastic bowl.

Leave to stand for 2-3 days. Taste to see if the mixture is sour. If not, leave it for another day to ferment.

When the mixture is ready, pour 750 ml (3 cups) water in a saucepan and heat to boiling point.

Gradually add the fermented mixture, stirring continuously to eliminate lumps. Cover and simmer for 30 minutes or until cooked. Serve with liver and morogo.

> **Maize-rice, a rice-shaped grain made from maize, is sometimes mixed into sour porridge (*ting*). Maize-rice is available from most supermarkets. Corn-rice is a type of crushed wheat. The grains are larger than maize-rice and are round.**

LEKHOTLOANE
Pounded Meat

SERVES 4-6

750 g-1 kg (1½–2½ lb) leg of lamb
1 litre (4 cups) water
45 ml (3 T) oil
2 onions, finely chopped
1 beef stock cube dissolved in 250 ml (1 cup)
    hot water
salt and pepper to taste

Boil the leg of lamb in the water until soft
and falling off the bone.

Cut the meat into portions and pound it
until it resembles stringy mince.

Heat the oil and sauté the onions until
transparent. Add the pounded meat and stock.

Simmer gently until the sauce thickens.
Season and serve with steam dumpling (see
the recipe for leqebekoane on page 42) and
morogo (see pages 38 and 43) or spinach.

LIKAHARE
Mixed Offal

SERVES 4-6

1 kg (2½ lb) mixed offal (tripe, intestines,
    lungs, etc.)
2 vegetable stock cubes, dissolved in 500 ml
    (2 cups) hot water
2 onions, sliced
salt and pepper to taste

Clean the offal thoroughly and rinse under
cold running water.

Heat the stock to boiling point and add the
meat. Cook gently for about 2 hours or until
the meat is tender.

Remove meat from the sauce and slice thinly.

Add the onions to the sauce, return the meat,
season and simmer for a further 30 minutes.

Serve warm on nyekoe with morogo (see
pages 38 and 43) or spinach.

NYEKOE
Corn Rice and Beans

SERVES 4-6

200 g (7 oz)/250 ml (1 cup) dry sugar beans
500 ml (2 cups) water
340 g (12 oz)/500 ml (2 cups) corn rice
60 g (2½ oz)/60 ml(4 T) butter/margarine
salt and pepper to taste

Place the sugar beans in a bowl and cover completely with water. Soak overnight. Drain.

In a saucepan, heat the water until it boils, add the beans and cook for 1 hour.

Add the corn rice, top up with water if necessary and cook gently for a further 1 hour.

Stir in the butter/margarine and season with salt and pepper to taste.

Steamed dumpling (page 42) is popular among all African tribes and each one has a special way of making it. *Leqebekoane* is made with fermented maize-meal paste to give it a musty taste. The paste is prepared by mixing maize-meal with water and leaving it for at least two days to ferment. This dumpling is always steamed separately in a basin, never over a stew.

LEQEBEKOANE
Steamed Dumpling

SERVES 4-6

360 g (12 oz)/(750 m) (3 cups) flour
120 g (4½ oz)/250 ml (1 cup) fermented
   maize-meal paste
1 packet (10 g) dry yeast
30 ml (2 T) sugar
5 ml (1 t) salt
1 egg, beaten
± 500 ml (2 cups) lukewarm water, or
   water mixed with milk

Sift the flour and mix in the dry ingredients.

Mix the egg with water. Add enough lukewarm water to the dry ingredients to form a soft and pliable dough. Knead for 10 minutes.

Cover the dough with plastic and leave to rise until doubled in size. Knock the dough down and place it in a greased enamel bowl. Allow to rise again until double in size before steaming.

Meanwhile, heat the water until it boils in a pot large enough to hold the bowl containing the dumpling. Immerse it in the hot water (the water should come half of the way up the sides of the dish). Seal the pot tightly and simmer gently for 1 hour. Try to avoid opening the saucepan during steaming. Replenish water if necessary.

TO SERVE: Cut the dumpling into wedges.

SECHU SAKHOHO
Chicken Stew

SERVES 4-6

1 whole chicken of 750 g–1 kg (1½–2½ lb)
60 ml (4 T) oil
2 onions, chopped
1 glove garlic, crushed
3 medium tomatoes, peeled and chopped
2 chillies, seeded and chopped
1 chicken stock cube, dissolved in 250 ml
   (1 cup) water
salt and pepper to taste

Cut the chicken into portions. Heat the oil and fry the chicken on all sides until brown.

Add the onions and garlic, and sauté until the onions are tender.

Add the tomatoes, chillies and stock. Season and simmer for 45-60 minutes.

Serve hot on pap (porridge) or mashed potatoes, with morogo (see pages 38 and 43) or spinach.

> **Morogo is a generic term for wild leaves. Leaves from the bean plant, beetroot leaves or sweet potato leaves can also be used for morogo.**

MOROGO WITH TURNIPS AND POTATOES

SERVES 4-6

2 bunches morogo
1 bunch spring onions, chopped
1 bunch turnips, peeled and diced
3 potatoes, peeled and diced
water
salt and pepper to taste
45 g (1½ oz)/45 ml (3 T) butter/
  margarine

Rinse morogo thoroughly and chop finely.

Place morogo, spring onions, turnips, potatoes and a little water in a saucepan. Season with salt and pepper.

Let it boil and then simmer gently for about 30 minutes until cooked.

Add the butter or margarine and mix well. Serve hot on pap.

BORDERED BY SOUTH AFRICA in the north, south and west, and by Mozambique in the east, Swaziland is one of the world's smallest countries. It sits on the edge of he southern African escarpment, with the rugged mountains in the west sloping down toward the low-lying plains in the east.

The Swazis, once part of the Dlamini clan, who were led across the Lebombo mountains in the mid-eighteenth century by Ngwane I, is one of very few remaining monarchies on the continent. Swaziland's first king, Sobhuza I, gathered refugees fleeing from the Zulu and merged these with his own people, thus building a strong military nation that managed to withstand the onslaught of Shaka. Taking their name from one of the founders of the nation, Mswati I, they waged wars against many neighbouring nations, but eventually succumbed to British rule, finally gaining their independence in 1968. The Swazis speak mainly isiSwati and English and are led today by King Mswati III, who is much revered by his people.

Even in the modern nation, it is quite common to see men and women draped in colourful traditional fabric, called *amahiya*, and the local craftmarkets also abound with the traditional regalia of a people fiercely protective of their cultural heritage.

Pulses are popular among the Swazi: round beans and lentils are cooked with maize-meal to prepare *lusontfwana* and *tinhlumaya nemphuphu* respectively. Boiled *tindlubu* (round beans) or *umbhonyo* (nuts) are cooled and then shelled and eaten. Maize is enjoyed in many forms: *imbasa* (half-dry roasted maize, mixed with dry nuts, which are then pan-fried), *tinkobe* (dried maize kernels cooked in salted water and allowed to cool before being eaten), and *lukhotse* (fried maize kernels with nuts that are ground and mixed with water). Another favourite is *tincheke*, boiled pumpkin wedges sprinkled with sugar.

ULUSU NAMAZAMBANE
Tripe and Potato Stew

SERVES 4-6

1 kg (2½ lb) tripe, washed and cut into pieces
water
4 potatoes, quartered
1 onion, chopped
15 ml (1 T) curry powder
5 ml (1 t) salt

Cover the tripe with water, bring to the boil and then simmer for 3 hours.

Add potatoes, onion, curry powder and salt.

Simmer for a further 30 minutes until the potatoes are cooked through. Serve with spinach porridge.

ISIJABANE
Spinach Porridge

SERVES 4

5 spinach leaves, cut into pieces
1 onion, grated
pinch of salt
1 litre (4 cups) water
240 g (9 oz)/500 ml (2 cups) maize-meal

Place the spinach in a saucepan, add the onion and salt, and cover with the water. Bring to the boil and cook for 5 minutes.

Add the maize-meal and stir to mix.

Simmer the porridge over a low heat for 30 minutes, stirring frequently until cooked. Serve with milk.

VARIATION: Diced pumpkin can be used instead of spinach.

SIDLWADLWA WITH SAMP
Meat and Vegetable Stew

SERVES 6-8

300 g (11 oz)/375 ml (1½ cups) samp
750 ml (3 cups) water
125 ml (½ cup) oil
1 kg (2½ lb) beef, cubed
3 tomatoes, choppedd
500 ml (2 cups) chopped cabbage
375 ml (1½ cups) crushed peanuts
salt and pepper to taste

Soak the samp overnight in cold water. Drain and cover with fresh water. Cook for about 1½ hours until soft.

In another pot, heat the oil and brown the beef. Add the tomatoes, cabbage and crushed peanuts. Season with salt and pepper. Stew for 15 minutes. Mix the stew with the samp. Serve with spinach porridge (see page 46).

SAMP AND BEANS WITH NUTS

SERVES 4

200 g (7 oz)/250 ml (1 cup) samp
200 g (7 oz)/250 ml (1 cup) dry butter beans
water
150 g (5 oz)/250 ml (1 cup) unsalted peanuts
3 chicken stock cubes
salt and pepper to taste
125 ml (½ cup) skim milk powder
75 g (3 oz)/75 ml (5 T) butter/margarine

Cover the samp and beans with water and soak overnight. Drain.

Place the samp, beans and nuts in a large saucepan and cover with water. Crumble the chicken stock cubes and add to the mixture. Let it boil and then simmer for 3 hours, adding more water if the samp becomes dry.

Season with salt and pepper. Add the milk powder and butter/margarine. Toss together or mash with a wooden spoon.

BEEF STEW

SERVES 4-6

60 ml (4 T) oil
750 g (1½ lb) shin, cut into cubes
45 ml (3 T) flour
salt and pepper to taste
2 onions, chopped
1 garlic glove, crushed
5 ml (1 t) ground cumin
5 ml (1 t) ground coriander
3 potatoes, diced
4 carrots, sliced
1 beef stock cube, dissolved in 500 ml
   (2 cups) water

Heat the oil, toss the meat in seasoned flour
and fry until brown on all sides. Remove the
meat and keep warm.

Add the onions, garlic, cumin and coriander
to the oil and sauté until transparent.

Add all the remaining ingredients and heat
until boiling. Reduce the heat and simmer for
about 45 minutes until cooked through. Serve
with samp (see page 47).

SISHWALA
Sugar Bean Porridge

SERVES 4

500 ml (2 cups) sugar beans
water
10 ml (2 t) salt
480 g (17 oz)/1 kg (2½ lb) maize-meal

Soak beans overnight in cold water.

Drain, cover with fresh water and add salt.
Cook in a large saucepan until soft.

Add maize-meal, mix well and cook for
30 minutes.

INDLANGALA
Carrot and Green Bean Soup

SERVES 4

80 ml (5 T) oil
2 carrots, diced
125 ml (½ cup) green beans
125 ml (½ cup) peanut butter
salt and pepper to taste
1 litre (4 cups) water

Heat oil. Add vegetables one at a time
and cook each for 2-3 minutes before adding
the next.

Add the peanut butter, salt and pepper.
Add water and cook over a low heat for
30 minutes.

THE NDEBELE, SOMETIMES REFERRED TO AS MATABELE, are a typical mixture of southern African cultures and this is evident in their blend of staple foods. Descended from the Nguni group – Zulu, Xhosa and Swazi – the Ndebele consist of three groups: one resident in Zimbabwe, and two in the northern provinces of South Africa. The first of the groups migrated from what is today KwaZulu-Natal in about 1600 and, more than two centuries later, another fled north of the Limpopo River. The man responsible for the exodus was Mzilikazi, one of Shaka's Zulu officers, who rebelled against his leader in 1821 and founded the kingdom of the Ndebele. The Ndebele consequently mixed with the Sotho and Afrikaners.

The nation is perhaps most noted for its exquisite artwork and striking houses with brilliantly painted walls. Many Ndebele women are gifted artists who have mastered the art of geometric design, most apparent in their traditional costume. They take great pride in their beadwork, and some women wear heavy neckbangles and anklets (*iingolwane*), and adorn themselves in colourful blankets.

One of my most vivid memories of growing up in the townships is the blanket-clad Ndebele women selling maize, *umseme* (mats), *umthanyelo* (short brooms) and hand-woven baskets. I also watched in fascination as my aunt, a traditional Ndebele woman, artistically plastered the floor with cow dung, each time executing a different pattern.

The basic Ndebele diet comprises largely maize, pumpkin and meat, *umbido* (beans) and *umratha* (Ndebele porridge). *Vetkoek,* of Dutch/Afrikaans origin, and called *amafetkuku* by the Ndebele is also popular. *Uburotho ne konfyt* (bread and jam) is a favourite snack. Marula beer is enjoyed during the marula (fruit) season, and like other traditional groups who, for centuries, relied on the land for their sustenance, the Ndebele continue to enjoy caterpillars, sand crickets, beetles, flying insects and termites. In summer, before the rain falls, flying ants emerge and are collected, grilled and eaten as a delicacy.

ULUSU NAMA DOMBOLO

Tripe and Sweetbreads with Dumplings

SERVES 4

1 kg (2½ lb) sheep offal (tripe, sweetbreads
  and intestines)
salt and pepper to taste

DUMPLINGS:
120 h (4½ oz)/250 ml (1 cup) wholewheat flour
1 packet (10 g) instant dry yeast
salt to taste
15 ml (1 T) lukewarm sugar water

Clean the offal and cut it into small pieces.
Place in a pot and cover with water.

Cook the offal over a moderate heat for
about 2 hours. Season with salt and pepper.

DUMPLINGS: Mix all the ingredients together.
Knead for 15 minutes until the dough is
elastic. Place the dough in a bowl, cover with
plastic and allow to rise in a warm place.

Roll the dough into balls the size of golf
balls. Place dough balls on meat 30 minutes
before the end of the cooking time. Cover
the saucepan and simmer until the meat and
dumplings are cooked through. Serve hot
with vegetables.

ITHANGA NESIPHILA
Pumpkin and Maize

SERVES 4

1 small pumpkin, cut into small pieces
fresh maize kernels, cut from 2 cobs
± 125 ml (½ cup) water
5 ml (1 t) sugar (optional)
pinch of salt (optional)

Put pumpkin, maize and water in a saucepan.

Cook for about 45 minutes, until the maize is
tender and the pumpkin is cooked. Stir to mix.

Add sugar and salt, if preferred.

DITLOO/IZINDLUBU
Jugo Beans

SERVES 4

2 kg (4½ lb) ditloo
500 ml (2 cups) water
salt to taste

Cook the ditloo in the water for about
30 minutes, until tender.

Season and serve in small bowls, like peanuts.

Ditloo or jugo beans are round,
shiny beans often simple referred
to as "traditional beans". They have
a rich, creamy taste and can be
served on their own as a snack, as
a side dish, or added to soups.

IDOMBOLO
Wholewheat Dumplings

SERVES 4

240 g (9 oz)/500 ml (2 cups) wholewheat
  flour (nutty wheat)
1 packet (10 g) instant dry yeast
5 ml (1 t) sugar
pinch of salt
± 250 ml (1 cup) lukewarm water

Sift the dry ingredients together in a large
mixing bowl.

Slowly add the lukewarm water and mix
well to form a soft, pliable dough.

Knead the dough well for 10 minutes, cover
with plastic and allow to rise for 45 minutes
until it has doubled in size.

Knock the dough down by kneading it, put
it in a greased enamel bowl and allow it to
rise again until double in size.

Place the bowl in a saucepan with boiling
water. Cover the saucepan tightly and steam
for 1 hour.

COW HEEL SOUP

SERVES 4-6

1 kg (2½ lb) cow trotters, cleaned and cut
  into portions (ask your butcher to clean
  and slice them)
2 litres (3½ pints/8 cups) water
1 kg (2½ lb) butter beans, soaked overnight
20ml (4 t) curry powder
salt and pepper to taste

Cover the trotters with the water and cook
for 1 hour or until half-cooked.

Add the butter beans, curry powder, salt
and pepper. Simmer for a further hour, until
the beans are tender, adding more water
if necessary. Serve hot with dumplings (see
page 52 and 53), bread or porridge.

UMQOMBOTHI (ITHLODLWA)
Sorghum Beer

MAKES 8 LITRES (14 PINTS)

6 kg (13½ lb) sorghum
3 kg (6½ lb) maize-meal
4 litres (7 pints) boiling water
4 litres (7 pints) cold water
1 packet (10 g) brewer's yeast

Mix 3 kg (6½ lb) sorghum with the maize-meal and add the boiling water. Leave to cool. Stir in 1 kg (2½ lb) sorghum. Allow the mixture to stand overnight.

Place the mixture in a large saucepan, add 1 litre (4 cups) cold water and boil together for 1 hour. Leave to cool.

When the mixture is cold, pour it into a large bucket and add the remaining 2 kg (4½ lb) sorghum. Add the rest of the cold water and mix well.

Add the brewer's yeast and stir to mix all the ingredients.

Cover the mixture with a piece of plastic or a damp cloth and allow to stand for at least 12 hours to brew.

Strain the mixture well. Serve cold.

SWEET-SOUR BEETROOT SALAD

SERVES 4-6

4 medium beetroot
1 small onion, grated
1 apple, grated
20 ml (4 t) mild chutney
80 g (3 oz)/100 ml (¼–½ cup) sugar
10 ml (2 t) cornflour
75 ml (5 T) vinegar
75 ml (5 T) water
pinch of salt

Wash the beetroot well and cook for 30-60 minutes, or until tender.

Put the cooked beetroot in cold water for a few minutes before removing the skins.

Dice or slice the beetroot and add the onion, apple and chutney.

Mix together the sugar, cornflour, vinegar, water and salt. Boil until the sauce thickens.

Pour the sauce over the beetroot and allow the salad to cool before serving.

Umqombothi is a popular African beer, associated with all forms of celebrations and casual drinking. It is highly intoxicating, and is enjoyed by adults only. Children are allowed a tiny sip only if there is an ancestral feast. The beverage that is enjoyed by the whole family is *mageu* (see page 60). Both *umqombothi* and *mageu* are readily availably from bottle stores and supermarkets.

CHAKALAKA SALAD

SERVES 4-6

50 ml (3 T) oil
1 onion, grated
2 garlic cloves, crushed
30 ml (2 T) crushed ginger
1 green pepper, deseeded and grated
3 green chillies, deseeded and chopped
10 ml (2 t) curry powder
3 medium carrots, grated
1 medium cauliflower, divided into florets
1 tin (410 g/14 oz) baked beans
salt and pepper to taste

Heat the oil and sauté the onion, garlic, ginger and green pepper with the chillies and curry powder for 5 minutes.

Add the carrots and cauliflower.

Cook gently for about 15 minutes or until all the vegetables are cooked.

Add the beans and seasoning, heat through and allow to cool.

Serve cold.

This salad is similar to atjar, and can be kept in the fridge for several days.

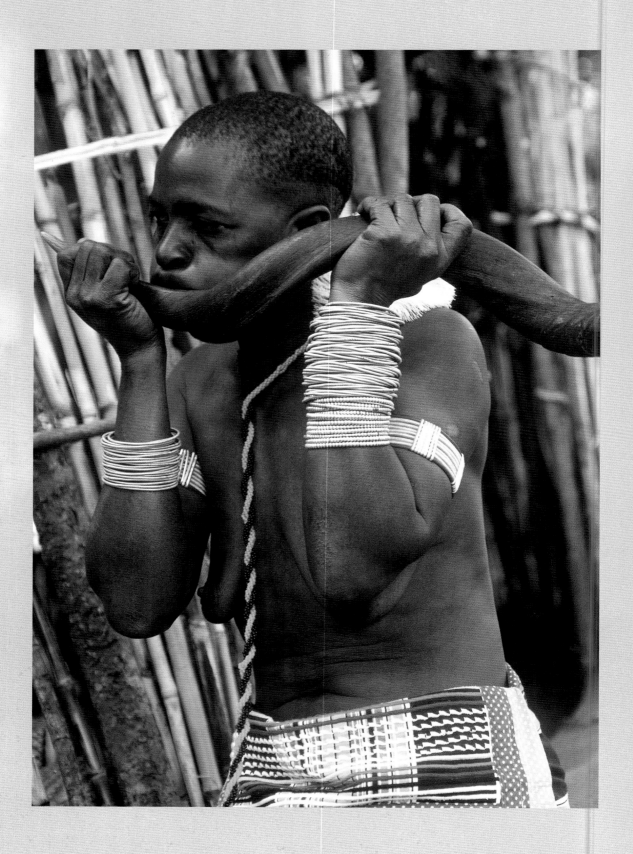

VENDA

VENDA

THE VHAVENDA LIVE in the northern part of Limpopo province. It is believed that they originally came from the Congo area, moved to present day Zimbabwe and a part of the group followed the mythic chief Thohoyandou ("head of the elephant") and crossed the Limpopo River. These gifted craftsmen smelted iron and created metal implements, which they used to cultivate the land rather than farm with cattle.

Venda food is simple, yet rich in flavour. *Dofhi* (peanut sauce) forms the basis of many dishes. *Mashonzha* (mopane worms), *tshisevho* (dried meat) and *mukusule* (wild leaves or morogo) are cooked in this piquant sauce and served with *vhutete* or *vhuswa* (porridge). Several herbs and spices such as *lunonya* (caraway seeds) and *mufhoho* (similar to mustard seeds) are grown in the region.

TSONGA

The Tsonga people live in areas extending from St Lucia Bay on the northern KwaZulu Natal coast, up to the Sabie River, they also leave in various districts of the Northern Province where they are interspersed with the Pedi in the west and the Venda and Lobedu in the north. A large community of Tsonga / Shangaan people can be found in the Mozambique province of Gaza. Tsonga indigenous food is very similar to Venda food, rich and full of flavour: dishes such as *matomani* (mopani worms), *tihove, tshopi, vuswa bya mavele, xigwimbi, vukanyi, xigugu* form the basics of Tsonga traditional food.

PEDI

The Pedi people arose out of a confederation of small chiefdoms in what later became the Northern Province. Many made their new home along the beautiful Soutpansberg Mountain Range, the same area that housed the Venda people and they called themselves the baPedi.

Traditional Pedi food consists of *thophi* (a meal which is made from maize mixed with a fruit called *lerotse*), *morogo wadikgopana* (spinach cooked and formed into lumps and dried in the sun). *Bogobe bam abele*, samp and *maswi* (milk), *masonja* (mopane worms) are also eaten as well as vegetables and fruits such as *milo* and *machilo*.

Traditionally, meat dried at home is used for this dish. If a lot of meat is left over after a celebration, it is cut into strips and dried in the sun for a few days. It is then kept and used when needed. Thick biltong can be used instead of home-dried meat.

TSHISEVHO
Dried Meat Stew

SERVES 4

500 g (18 oz) dried meat (biltong)
rough salt to taste
250 ml (1 cup) water
125 ml (½ cup) ground nuts (peanuts crushed
  in a traditional pestle and mortar, and sifted)

Cook the pieces of dried meat in salted water until soft. Remove and keep warm.

Add the ground nuts to the meat stock, stirring continuously until a smooth sauce is formed.

Return the cooked dried meat to the pot and heat through to blend the flavours.

DRIED MUKUSULE WITH DOFHI
Dried Morogo with Peanut Sauce

SERVES 4

1 kg (2½ lb) dried mukusule leaves
250 ml (1 cup) water
salt and pepper to taste

DOFHI:
125 ml (½ cup) ground nuts
250 ml (1 cup) water

Rinse the mukusule under cold running water and drain.

Place the mukusule in a saucepan with the water and cook until soft.

In the meantime, make the *dofhi* by simmering the ground nuts in the water for 15 minutes until creamy.

Mix the *mukusule* into the ground nut sauce and simmer gently to combine the flavours. Season with salt and pepper.

A variety of wild leaves are used as *mukusule* – even greens from the bean plant, beetroot or pumpkin. If there are excess leaves, they are sun dried and kept for future use, especially during the winter months.

MASHONZHA
Mopane Worms with Tomato and Onion Stew

SERVES 4

250 ml (1 cup) dried mopane worms
500 ml (2 cups) hot water
500 ml (2 cups) boiling water
20 ml (4 t) cooking oil
1 medium onion, chopped
salt and pepper to taste
2 medium tomatoes, diced
pinch of chilli powder

Soak the dried mopane worms in hot water for about 3 hours.

Remove the mopane worms from the water and place them in a saucepan.

Add the boiling water and cook until most of the water has be absorbed.

Add oil and onion, season with salt and pepper, and simmer for about 5 minutes.

Add the tomatoes and chilli powder, cover and simmer for 10 minutes.
Serve hot with fermented porridge.

VARIATION: Replace the onion stew with peanut sauce (*dofhi*).

FERMENTED VHUSWA
Porridge

SERVES 4

360 g (12 oz)/750 ml (3 cups) super maize-meal
1 litre (4 cups) lukewarm water
1 litre (4 cups) boiling water
1 kg (2½ lb) special maize-meal

Soak the super maize-meal in lukewarm water, cover and leave to ferment for 2 days.

Pour boiling water into a saucepan and add 500 ml (2 cups) of the fermented water.

Bring the water to the boil and add the fermented maize-meal paste. Simmer gently, stirring until the mixture thickens.

Cover the saucepan and cook the mixture over a low heat for 10 minutes. Add small quantities of the special maize-meal, mixing thoroughly to avoid lumps.

Cover and simmer for a further 15 minutes, stirring the porridge constantly.

> **Super maize-meal is ordinary refined maize-meal, which is sold in most supermarkets. Special maize-meal is commonly referred to as 'No. 1'and is available from selected shops. It is highly refined and looks a lot like flour.**

VHUTETWE/VHUSWA

1 litre (4 cups) water
240 g (9 oz)/500 ml (2 cups) maize-meal

Bring the water to the boil and slowly add the maize-meal. Stir thoroughly with a whisk until smooth.

Pound the mixture with a wooden spoon to ensure that no lumps remain. Cook for about 20 minutes, pounding and stirring, until the porridge is cooked through.

Pour layers of hot porridge on a plate to resemble stacked thick pancakes. Leave the porridge to cool and eat it with your hand.

SPINACH AND MUKUSULE MIX

SERVES 4

1 bunch spinach leaves
1 bunch beetroot leaves
1 bunch pumpkin leaves
1 large potato, quartered
1 large onion, chopped
250 ml (1 cup) water
60 ml (4 T) butter/margarine
salt and masala to taste

Wash the leaves thoroughly, rinse, chop and place in a saucepan.

Add the potato, onion, water, salt and masala. Cook for 20 minutes or until the potato is soft.

Add butter/margarine. Mash until well mixed.

MAGEU

MAKES 1 LITRE (1½ PINTS)

750 ml (3 cups) water
120 g (4½ oz)/250 ml (1 cup) maize-meal
60 ml (4 T) flour
sugar to taste

Boil the water in a saucepan.

Mix a little cold water with the maize-meal to make a paste.

Add the paste to the boiling water and stir to mix. Turn down the heat and simmer gently, stirring constantly until cooked. Leave to cool.

Add the flour and sugar, mix well and leave to stand for two days.

Taste to see whether the mixture is sour. If not, leave it to stand for another day. Dilute with water, if necessary, and then serve.

Usually "Special No. 1" maize-meal is used for this porridge. The porridge is cooked in the morning and kept all day. The layers come off easily and the porridge is kept covered so that it stays moist. It is eaten with *mukusule* (morogo) and *mashonza* (mopane worms) and meat stews.

CHICKEN-FEET STEW

SERVES 4-6

6 chicken feet, cleaned
6 chicken heads, cleaned
500 g (18 oz) chicken
    intestines, cleaned
water
45 ml (3 T) oil
1 green pepper, seeded and
    chopped
1 large tomato, grated
salt and masala to taste

Cover the meat with water and heat until boiling. Lower the heat and simmer gently for about 30 minutes until cooked.

Heat the oil and fry the green pepper until soft. Add the tomato, salt and masala.

Add the tomato gravy to the meat and simmer for 15 minutes.

Serve with potato *pap* (porridge) or dumplings (see recipes for *ulusu nama dombolo* and *idombolo* on pages 52 and 53).

COOKING FROM
CAPE **TO**
CAIRO
BOTSWANA

LANDLOCKED BOTSWANA, surrounded by Zimbabwe, South Africa and Namibia, is a thriving country, rich in diamonds, wildlife and talented, friendly people. The small eastern section that includes part of the Limpopo River is home to 80 percent of the Batswana. The land here is extremely fertile, whereas the huge western area is mostly too dry for dependable agriculture and cannot, therefore, sustain any more than a sparse population. Rainfall throughout the country is both sparse and erratic, and Botswana is frequently plagued by drought.

The first Tswana speakers, the Kwena, entered what is now Botswana from the south in the eighteenth century, but the Ngwaketse and the Ngwato soon broke away. The Tswana, in turn, then broke from the Ngwato, and by the nineteenth century the Tswana were well established in the area. Botswana finally gained its independence from Britain in 1966, and it has remained a largely tranquil country, where the government functions on democratic principles. This relative calm has since given rise to exciting developments in

the tourist industry, which is built around the country's abundant wildlife resources, most notably in the northern regions.

Most Batswana generally hold other people in high regard and believe a man's worth is measured by the way he treats others (*motho ke motho ka batho*).

The Setswana diet consists mainly of *bogobe*, *legola* (grain sorghum), and *sebube* (grain sorghum porridge cooked in sour milk). *Ting* (fermented porridge) made from plain maize meal or *mabele* meal is also a firm favourite, while chopped *diretlo lserobe* (tripe), *seswaa* (pounded meat) and *phane* (mopane worms) are popular accompaniments to the meal. As with most African groups, *morogo* is eaten in abundance, the most popular version being made from leaves of the bean plant. *Dinawa* (dried beans), *ditloo* (jugo beans) and *letlhodi* (lentils), boiled in salted water and seasoned with salt and pepper, also form part of the daily Setswana menu.

SESWAA
Pounded Meat

SERVES 6

1 kg (2½ lb) brisket
1 large onion, chopped
salt and pepper to taste
water

Place the brisket, the onion and seasoning in a saucepan. Cover with water and cook about 2½ hours until soft.

Drain liquid and pound the meat until flaky. Remove the bones. Serve with porridge (see page 59), *morogo* and gravy.

MOROGO

SERVES 4

1 kg (2½ lb) bean leaves
2 onions, chopped
125 ml (½ cup) water
15 ml (1 T) oil
salt and pepper to taste

Place the *morogo* and chopped onions in a saucepan and add the water and oil.

Boil for 15 minutes, stirring continuously. Season with salt and pepper.

VENISON RAGOUT

SERVES 4-6

1 leg of impala, approximately 750 g–1 kg (1½–2½ lb), deboned and cut into cubes
2 onions, chopped
2 ripe tomatoes, grated
62,5 ml (½ cup) oil
250 ml (1 cup) beef stock
salt and pepper to taste
250 g (½ lb) button mushrooms
50 ml (4 T) red wine
1 litre (4 cups) cream
30 ml (2 T) cranberry sauce, optional
chopped fresh parsley as garnish

Combine the cubed impala, onions, tomatoes, oil and stock. Simmer for 1 hour until soft.

Remove the meat from the stock and place in another saucepan. (Keep stock to make soup.) Season. Add the mushrooms, red wine and cream.

Cook slowly until creamy and thickened. Spoon into a serving dish, garnish with chopped parsley and cranberry sauce.

Serve with rice and vegetables in season.

For *morogo*, use plant leaves, preferably bean plants. The leaves are blanched and then sun dried. Shops in Botswana sell dried bean leaves.

TRADITIONAL SCONES

MAKES 12

240 g (9 oz)/500 ml (2 cups) cake flour
20 ml (4 t) baking powder
pinch of salt
80 ml (6 T) sugar
125 g (4½ oz)/125 ml (½ cup) butter/margarine
1 egg
150 ml (½ cup) milk

Preheat the oven to 220 °C (425 °F/gas 7).

Sift together the flour, baking powder and salt. Add the sugar and rub the butter/margarine into the mixture until it resembles breadcrumbs.

Beat the egg and milk together, gradually add the mixture to the flour and mix to make a pliable soft dough.

Roll the dough out lightly until it is about 10 mm (½ in) thick. Cut into scone shapes with a dough cutter.

Place on a grease baking sheet. Bake for 12-15 minutes.

> These scones differ from the cream and jam type – they are heavier due to the method of mixing. They are usually enjoyed with ginger beer.

GINGER BEER

MAKES 5 LITRES (8½ PINTS)

5 litres (8½ pints) boiling water
240 g (8 oz)/300 ml (1½ cup) sugar
30 ml (2 T) ground ginger
10 ml (2 t) active dry yeast, optional
15 ml (1 T) tartaric acid
15 ml (1 T) cream of tartar
250 ml (1 cup) raisins

Pour the boiling water into a large saucepan. Add sugar, stir to dissolve and add the ginger. Simmer for about 30 minutes. Leave until lukewarm.

Add the remaining ingredients. Cover and keep in a warm place for 2 days to mature. Chill before serving.

BOHOBE BATING YAMABELE
Sour Porridge

SERVES 4

2,5 litres (4½ pints/10 cups) water
4 x 250 ml (4 cups) fermented
ting paste

Heat the water to boiling point, pour half the *ting* paste into the boiling water and stir constantly to avoid lumps.

When the paste is smooth, let it cook slowly for about 10 minutes, stirring occasionally.

Add the rest of the paste. Cook for a further 30 minutes, stirring constantly. Serve with *morogo* (see pages 39, 43 and 64) or meat.

Mosoko, ting or sour porridge is a typical Batswana meal. To prepare *ting* paste, take any quantity of super maize meal or *mabele a ting* and mix with warm water. Cover and leave to ferment overnight.

OSTRICH KEBABS

SERVES 4-6

500 g (18 oz) ostrich fillet, cubed
2 onions, chopped
3 green peppers, chopped
salt and pepper to taste
250 ml (1 cup) bought pepper sauce
cranberry sauce (optional)

Thread the ostrich fillet, onions and peppers onto skewers.
Season with salt and pepper.

Grill the kebabs over medium heat for about 10 minutes.

Mix the pepper sauce with cranberry sauce, if preferred, and serve
over the kebabs. Serve the kebabs with rice and vegetables in season.

The ostrich is the largest bird in the world. In the early 1900s it was farmed extensively for its feathers. Due to changes in fashion, the industry died out. However, renewed interest in ostrich products have seen a revival in recent years. Now every part of the bird is used – the skin for leather, the feathers for fashion, and the eggshells for ornaments. The meat is very low in cholesterol and is extremely nutritious. Ostrich eggs – one is the equivalent of 24 large chicken eggs – are very rich.

ZIMBABWE

THIS LANDLOCKED COUNTRY lies entirely within the tropics and has been blessed with a balmy climate. Rainfall blows in from the east, drenching the spectacular highlands, but diminishes as the moist air moves west. Zimbabwe has been equally blessed with a rich and proud cultural history. There are many Stone Age rock paintings, and archaeologists can trace humankind's occupation of what is now Zimbabwe to 100 000 years ago. By the twelfth century, the Shona people were building with stone, initiating a unique African tradition that left Great Zimbabwe Ruins and other megalithic sites scattered around the country.

The Shona constitute some 75 per cent of the total population of around 8 million. The second largest group are the Nguni-speaking Ndebele, who, led by Mzilikazi, made their grand entrance into Zimbabwe around the nineteenth century and established themselves around Bulawayo.

Boasting the world-famous Victoria Falls, the great Zambezi River, Kariba and some of

Africa's finest game parks, the people of Zimbabwe are also some of the continent's most creative, and most of the rural folk are expert crafters. As an example, Sonile Ncube supports her family by selling the *hoso* (musical instruments) she finely crafts from fruit known as *umkhemeswane.* Her elder son carves hippos and other animals from wood, and the younger siblings smooth and polish them.

The staple diet of most Zimbabweans is *sadza* (porridge) made from maize-meal, with *rape* (a type of wild leaf) and *okra* as common side dishes, while nuts – ground and whole – form a major part of the menu.

Kapenta, a tiny fish found mainly in the Zambezi, is eaten throughout the country, as is *amacimbi* (mopane worms). Both are sun dried and stored until needed, and are prepared in much the same way: sautéed in oil and served on *sadza* or added to a tomato-and-onion stew.

NYAMA
Traditional Beef Stew

SERVES 4

1 kg (2½ lb) brisket or chuck, cut into portions
salt to taste
500 ml (2 cups) water
2 onions, chopped
2 tomatoes, chopped
salt and pepper to taste
4 x 250 ml (4 cups) *rape* or *chimolia*
  (*morogo*), shredded

Boil the meat in salted water until it is
cooked and soft.

Add the onion and tomato, salt and pepper,
and *rape* or *chimolia (morogo)*.

Simmer gently for about 20 minutes until the
vegetables are cooked through. Serve with
sadza, the Zimbabwean version of porridge
(see the recipe for *nshima* on page 86 for the
Zambian version).

PUMPKIN
IN PEANUT SAUCE

SERVES 4

125 ml (½ cup) water
½ pumpkin, peeled and cut into small portions
60 ml (4 T) peanut butter

Heat the water in a saucepan to boiling
point and add the pumpkin. Cook until soft,
stirring occasionally.

Add the peanut butter and stir to mix.
Mash until smooth.

CHUMUKUYU
Dried Meat

1 kg (2½ lb) lean sirloin of beef
10 ml (2 t) salt
5 ml (1 t) black pepper
5 ml (1 t) cayenne pepper
3 ml (½ t) peri peri
60 ml (4 T) olive oil

Preheat the oven to 140 °C (275 °F/gas 1).

Remove the gristle and sinew from the meat. Cut the meat into strips.

Lay the meat on a baking tray and season it with salt, black pepper, cayenne pepper and peri peri. Drizzle the olive oil over the meat.

Place the baking tray in the preheated oven, and leave the meat to dry for 30 minutes. Leave outside for at least 12 hours to dry completely. Serve as a snack.

CHUMUKUYU STEW
Dried Meat Stew

SERVES 4

12 pieces of dried meat, 300-500 g (11-18 oz)
water
60 g (2½ oz)/60 ml (4 T) butter/margarine
1 onion, sliced
1 garlic clove, crushed
4 ripe tomatoes, chopped
salt and pepper to taste
75 ml (5 T) peanut butter
1 packet of beef soup powder
250 ml (1 cup) water

Cover the dried meat with water and cook until tender.

Melt the butter/margarine and sauté the onion and garlic until transparent, Add the tomatoes. Season with salt and pepper.

Mix together the peanut butter, soup powder and water. Add the mixture to the stew and simmer gently for 5 minutes.

Add the cooked beef to the stew and mix well. Cook for 10 minutes until the flavours are blended. Serve on *sadza* (stiff porridge; see the recipe for *nshima* on page 86 for the Zambian version) or dumplings (see page 53) with fried brown mushrooms.

OKRA IN PEANUT SAUCE

SERVES 4

125 ml (½ cup) water
250 g (9 oz) fresh okra, sliced
2 ml (½ t) bicarbonate of soda
1 large tomato, grated
salt and pepper to taste
75 ml (5 T) pounded roasted peanuts

Heat the water to boiling point, add the okra and bicarbonate of soda. Cook for 10 minutes. Add the tomato, salt and pepper.

Mix the peanuts with a little water, add it to the okra and cook for a further 15 minutes. Serve with porridge (see the recipe for *vhuswa* on page 60).

Okra is a popular vegetable in most parts of Africa. The small variety is nicer for cooking. This vegetable is very nutritious and is best eaten with *sadza* (porridge).

CREAMY SWEET POTATOES

SERVES 4-6

4 sweet potatoes
water
125 ml (½ cup) whipped cream
1 tin (397 g/14 oz) condensed milk
62,5 ml (¼ cup) raisins

Rinse the sweet potatoes under running water. Place them in a saucepan, cover with water and boil in a saucepan, cover with water and boil in their jackets until cooked.

Peel the cooked sweet potatoes and mash until smooth.

Stir in the whipped cream, condensed milk and raisins. Serve with more whipped cream or custard for an unusual, delicious desert.

MAWUYU, UMKHOMO
Baobab Fruit in Cream

SERVES 4-6

8 baobab fruits
125 ml (½ cup) milk
100 g (4 oz)/125 ml (½ cup) sugar
250 ml (1 cup) whipped cream

Break the baobab fruits in half. Remove the floury seeds and place the fruit in a bowl.

Add the milk, sugar and whipped cream to form a thick consistency. Serve as dessert.

CHICKEN IN PEANUT SAUCE

SERVES 4-6

1 whole chicken of 750 g–1 kg
   (1½–2½ lb)
45 ml (3 T) seasoned flour
60 ml (4 T) oil
1 large onion, chopped
1 garlic clove, crushed
15 ml (1 T) crushed ginger
1 green pepper, chopped
2 large tomatoes, peeled and diced
1 chicken stock cube, dissolved in
   250 ml (1 cup) water
salt and pepper to taste
5 ml (1 t) rosemary
200 g (7 oz)/125 ml (½ cup)
   peanut butter

Cut the chicken into portions and toss in the seasoned flour.

Heat the oil and brown the chicken. Remove the chicken from the saucepan and keep warm.

Sauté the onion, garlic and ginger until transparent.

Add the green pepper and tomatoes. Return chicken to saucepan. Add stock, seasoning and rosemary. Bring to the boil and then simmer for 30 minutes.

Add the peanut butter and continue to cook over a low heat for a further 15 minutes. Add a little water if the stew is too thick. Serve with porridge (see the recipe for *vhuswa* on page 60).

MOZAMBIQUE'S LONG LANGUID SHORELINE stretches over 2 000 kilometres along the Indian Ocean, while the interior extends along the Zambezi valley to Zimbabwe and Zambia, with the southern tip of Malawi driving a wedge into Mozambican territory. Two of Africa's major rivers also flow through Mozambique.

During the country's wet season, it is both hot and humid, with temperatures rising up to 29 °C on the coast. The dry season runs from April to September, and it is during these months that the temperature is the most pleasant.

Although the Portuguese first arrived here as long ago as the fifteenth century, their early activities were restricted to setting up trading enclaves and forts along the coast, and the interior remained largely unblemished by colonial influence.

The indigenous communities mostly occupied the inland regions and conducted vigorous trading systems of their own. It was thus only in the seventeenth century that colonisation began to infiltrate, with private owners settling on land granted by the crown of Portugal or taken by the conquest of African chiefs.

Mozambique finally gained its independence from Portugal in 1975, but after so many years of colonial rule, the Portuguese and indigenous cultures have become intertwined and the country's official language remains Portuguese. Most Mozambican cafés and restaurants serve Portuguese food, and the Portuguese influence is also evident in the food eaten by the local people.

As in most African communities, porridge, called *nsima* in Mozambique, is the staple dish, closely followed by the ever-popular rice, most often combined with prawns and called *chiru* (pilau). *Chiguinha* is a mixture of cassava flour and ground peanuts, which are mixed together and simmered over a gentle heat.

BIFE A CARDOSO
Beef Cardoso Style

SERVES 1

250 ml (1 cup) water
300 g (11 oz) rump steak
1 medium onion
1 medium carrot
1 bay leaf
salt and pepper to taste
250 g (9 oz) white cabbage, sliced
20 ml (4 t) olive oil
300 g (11 oz) potatoes
2 eggs, fried
black olives for garnish

Boil 125 ml (½ cup) of the water. Add the meat, onion, carrot and bay leaf. Season and cook for 20 minutes.

Boil cabbage with 10 ml (2 t) of the olive oil.

Boil the potatoes in 125 ml water.

Slice the beef into three equal pieces, arrange on the bed of cabbage, alternating with the two fried eggs, and drizzle rest of olive oil over.

Serve with boiled potatoes, and the carrots and onion from the stock. Garnish with black olives.

A typical Mozambican dish, in which the Portuguese influence is evident.

GALINHA A PIRI PIRI
Peri Peri Chicken

SERVES 2

1 chicken of approximately 1,3 kg (2½ lb)
salt and pepper
200 g (7 oz)/200 ml (½ cup) butter
6 whole fresh peri peri or hot chillies, crushed
20 ml (4 t) lemon juice
4 cloves garlic, crushed
5 ml (1 t) paprika
20 ml (4 t) olive oil

SAUCE:
20 g (1 oz)/20 ml (4 t) butter
10 ml (2 t) olive oil
2 cloves garlic
ground peri peri to taste
juice of 1 lemon
15 ml (1 T) chopped parsley

Clean chicken, cut through back and flatten. Remove the carcass. Slit through the thick parts.

Mix the rest of ingredients to a paste. Rub it over the inside and outside of the chicken.

Marinate the chicken for 2 hours, then grill or braai, basting and turning it frequently.

SAUCE: Fry garlic in butter and olive oil. Add rest of ingredients. Remove garlic, pour sauce over chicken and serve with rice and vegetables.

CAMARÃO GRELHADO MATAPA

Morogo with Prawns

SERVES 4

1 kg (2½ lb) *matapa*, rinsed and chopped
100 g (4 oz) peanuts, crushed
250 ml (1 cup) coconut milk
4 tomatoes, peeled and chopped
1 onion, chopped
250 g (9 oz) dried prawns or shrimps

Mix all the ingredients in a saucepan.

Stew together until the matapa has cooked through. Serve over *nsima,* the Mozambican porridge (see the recipe for *nshima* on page 86 for the Zambian version).

Coconut milk is made by breaking open a whole fresh coconut and shredding the coconut flesh. Mix it with cold water and leave for a few minutes, then squeeze it through a strainer. Alternatively, place desiccated coconut in water and simmer gently. Rub the mixture through a sieve and use the fluid as coconut milk.

MUTHUMBULA/ MANDIOCA

Cassava

SERVES 4

250 g (9 oz) cassava
2 eggs, beaten
salt and pepper to taste
oil for frying

Peel and cut the cassava into serving portions. Boil until soft and cooked through.

Dip the cassava in beaten egg and deep-fry in hot oil. Serve as a side dish.

CAMARÃO GRELHADO
Grilled Prawns with Garlic Sauce

SERVES 1

12 medium-sized prawns
15 ml (1 T) lemon juice
10 ml (2 t) salt
5 whole peri peri or hot chillies,
   crushed
4 garlic cloves, crushed
20 ml (4 t) olive oil

GARLIC SAUCE:
125 g (4½ oz)/125 ml (½ cup) butter
2 cloves garlic, crushed
2 whole peri peri or hot chillies
1 bay leaf
25 ml (2 T) lemon juice

Slit the back of each prawn and devein.

Mix the lemon juice, salt, peri peri, garlic and olive oil
to a paste, press the paste into the cut of the prawn
and close. Sprinkle any remaining paste over the prawns
and marinate for 3 hours.

Grill the prawns for 20 minutes, using the marinade
for basting.

SAUCE: Melt the butter in a pan, add the garlic, peri peri
and bay leaf, and heat until boiling.

Remove from heat, add lemon juice and mix well. Serve
the prawns and garlic sauce with rice.

Cassava, a tubular vegetable that looks like a sweet potato, is used in many East and West African dishes. The peel is slit down to the flesh and pulled away with the fingers, like a ripe banana. The tuber is washed, rinsed and sliced lengthways to remove the core. Plain boiled cassava may replace potatoes in any meal. A variety of savoury and sweet dishes are made from whole cassava or cassava flour.

SAFFRON RICE SALAD TOPPED WITH MIXED SEAFOOD

SERVES 8

SAFFRON RICE:
4 threads saffron
250 ml (1 cup) lukewarm water
½ onion, chopped
15 ml (1 T) butter/margarine
150 g (5 oz)/187,5 ml (¾ cup) basmati
   rice
62,5 ml (¼ cup) wild rice
250 ml (1 cup) salted water

TOPPING:
45 ml (3 T) olive or sunflower oil
500 g (18 oz) selection of seafood
1 clove garlic, crushed
80 ml (5 T) white wine
salt and pepper to taste
15 ml (1 T) chopped capers
chopped dill

DRESSING:
60 ml (4 T) balsamic vinegar
15 ml (1 T) water
salt and pepper to taste
90 ml (6 T) olive oil

GARNISH:
100 g (4 oz) cherry tomatoes
½ cucumber, sliced

Mix saffron with 250 ml (1 cup) lukewarm water and set aside.

Melt the butter/margarine and lightly sauté the onion. Add the basmati rice and fry together for a few seconds.

Add the saffron water and salt and heat until boiling, stirring constantly. Cover until the rice is cooked. Remove from the heat and let it cool.

Meanwhile boil the wild rice in the salted water or approximately 20 minutes. Rinse with cold water and drain.

TOPPING: Heat the oil in a casserole. Add the seafood mix and crushed garlic, stir to cover and then roast the mixture under strong heat for 1 minute. Add the wine and seasoning. Cover the casserole and cook for 3 minutes. Remove the seafood mix and allow to cool.

DRESSING: Mix vinegar and 15 ml (1 T) water, season with salt and pepper and whisk in the oil.

Mix the saffron rice and wild rice together. Top with the seafood mix, capers and dill.

Refrigerate for 1 hour. Leave on the chilled platter, and before serving pour the dressing over and garnish with cherry tomatoes and cucumber slices.

Mozambique has an extremely long coastline with a warm coastal current, which creates an ideal breeding ground for a variety of shellfish. Not surprisingly, prawns feature prominently on their menu and "LM" prawns are a delicacy famous for both their size and flavour.

COOKING FROM

CAPE TO CAIRO

ZAMBIA

LANDLOCKED IN THE TROPICS of southern Africa, far from the shores of either the Atlantic or the Indian Oceans, lies the Republic of Zambia. Situated on a plateau between 900 and 1 500 metres above sea level, Zambia is studded with lakes and covered with deciduous forest, savanna and marshland, while its rivers and lakes provide abundant fish harvests. Zambia is blessed with exceptional beauty, and few other countries can boast such diversity. The Victoria Falls, the abundance of mountains, lakes, rivers, forests and wildlife typify Africa and make it extremely alluring to the visitor.

Signs of human habitation here go back some 200 000 years, with the earliest tribes gathering fruits, hunting and fishing to sustain themselves. They were, however, taken under British rule until the country gained its independence in 1964.

The Zambian population currently stands at nearly 10 million and although the country's official language remains English, there are a number of indigenous languages, including Bemba (the largest of the groups), Lozi, Nyanja and Tonga. However, despite over 70 different ethnic groups, Zambia is perhaps less affected by ethnic tensions than any African state.

Zambia is one of Africa's most urbanised countries, but while Lusaka is characterised by buzzing markets, the rural population live largely by subsistence farming. The country has an exotic cuisine, with extraordinary flavours and aromas. Its markets – the nerve centre where virtually the entire community shops – are brimming with all sorts of unusual vegetables. It is here that you will inevitably find fresh produce, live chickens, fresh fish, cooked food, crafts, jewellery and one of Zambia's most renowned exports, the colourful fabric known as *xhitenge*. During my visit to the country, a local housewife showed me how to cook *nshima* (porridge), chicken stew, *lumanda* (okra in peanut sauce), and introduced me to the flavours of Zambian beverages, such as *muukhoyo, tombwa* and *kachasu*.

VENISON SHIN

SERVES 6-8

45 ml (3 T) oil
2 kg (4½ lb) shin, cut into thin slices
3 onions, chopped
4 tomatoes, chopped
500 ml (2 cups) water
salt and pepper to taste

Heat the oil and brown the meat.

Add the onions and tomatoes, sauté for a few minutes and add the water. Allow to simmer for 1½ hours, stirring occasionally.

Season with salt and pepper, and reduce the sauce by boiling uncovered. Serve on rice or stiff porridge.

NSHIMA
Stiff Porridge

SERVES 6-8

5 litres (8½ pints) water
salt to taste (optional)
240 g (9 oz)/500 ml (2 cups) maize-meal

Heat the water to boiling point. Add salt, if preferred. Gradually add the maize-meal, stirring all the time until it is mixed with the water.

Cover and allow to cook over medium heat until cooked through, stirring constantly to avoid burning.

Porridge is a staple food in most of Africa. It may be prepared in many different ways, which result in a variety of textures, but the basic ingredients remain the same. The amount of water used determines the consistency. For soft porridge, which is served at breakfast, use twice the amount of water as that required for stiff porridge. This stiff porridge, known as *nshima* in Zambia and Malawi, is served at lunch and dinner.

NKUKU
Chicken

SERVES 8-10

3 kg (6½ lb) chicken
salt and pepper to taste
200 ml (½ cup) oil
1 large onion, chopped
2 large tomatoes, chopped

Cut the chicken into portions. Season with salt and pepper.

Heat the oil and cook the chicken until brown. Add the onion and brown.

Stir in the tomatoes, turn down the heat and stew for 45 minutes. Serve with stiff porridge and sweet potato leaves (see the recipe for *kalembula,* on page 88).

ANGWALA
Whole Bream

SERVES 8

60 g (2½ oz)/125 ml (½ cup) flour
salt and pepper to taste
4 whole breams
60 ml (4 T) lemon juice
125 ml (½ cup) oil
2 onions, sliced
4 tomatoes, peeled and chopped
2 fresh chillies

Mix together the flour, salt and pepper. Brush the fish with the lemon juice and coat with the seasoned flour.

Heat the oil in a pan. Pan-fry the fish on both sides for about 10 minutes, or until it is brown and crisp.

Place the fried fish on a serving dish and keep it warm.

In another pan, mix together the onions, tomatoes and chillies and fry until soft.

Serve the fish with the tomato sauce and rice.

Use any firm white fish, such as hake, as a substitute for *angwala*.

KALEMBULA
Sweet Potato Leaves

SERVES 4

500 ml (2 cups) water
3 ripe tomatoes, peeled and chopped
750 ml (3 cups) sweet potato leaves
salt and pepper to taste

Boil the water, add the tomatoes and cook until soft.

Add sweet potato leaves and cook 10 minutes more. Season with salt and pepper. Serve with porridge (see recipe for *nshima,* page 86).

VARIATION: Make a sauce using freshly ground peanuts and boiling water, add it to the leaves and simmer for 20 minutes. This dish is called *mbyori*.

FUTARI
Baked Sweet Potatoes

SERVES 8

6 x 250 ml (6 cups) water
2 kg (4½ lb) sweet potatoes, peeled and thinly sliced
salt to taste

PEANUT SAUCE:
4 x 250 ml (4 cups) ground nuts
250 ml (1 cup) hot water

Boil water in a saucepan. Add sweet potatoes and cook until soft. Drain. Arrange the slices in a baking dish. Season with salt and keep warm.

PEANUT SAUCE: Combine the ground nuts and hot water in a small bowl.

Pour the sauce on the sweet potatoes and bake at 180 °C (350 °F/gas 4) for 15 minutes.

IMPHWA
Baby Brinjal

SERVES 8

500 ml (2 cups) water
3 onions, chopped
3 tomatoes, chopped
750 ml (3 cups) diced brinjal
Salt and pepper to taste
3 ml (½ t) chilli powder
3 ml (½ t) turmeric

Boil the water in a saucepan, add the onions and tomatoes, and simmer for 10 minutes.

Add rest of ingredients. Cook for 20 minutes. Serve with porridge (see *nshima* on page 86).

DELELE
Okra

SERVES 6

500 ml (2 cups) water
5 ml (1 t) bicarbonate of soda
750 ml (3 cups) okra, sliced
3 tomatoes, peeled and chopped
salt and pepper to taste

Bring water to the boil, then add bicarbonate of soda. When dissolved, add the okra, tomatoes and seasoning. Simmer for 15 minutes, stirring occasionally.

When the okra boils over, it's cooked and ready for serving. Serve with porridge (see the recipe for *nshima* on page 86).

MALAWI LIVES UP TO its reputation as "the warm heart of Africa". Situated along the southern continuation of the great Rift Valley, Malawi consists of a narrow sliver that is densely populated. Its small size and irregular borders are remnants of late nineteenth-century politics that played havoc with the internal affairs of the continent.

Although much of the land is covered with forest and savanna, fishing remains the main industry and major source of income for the people who live along the shore of Lake Malawi, Lake Chilwa and the Shire River. A plantation economy produces tobacco, cotton, tea and groundnuts for export.

The population is over 11 million, but many of the adult males labour on the mines and tobacco farms accross the borders. English and Chewa are the official languages.

The markets sell virtually everything, from exotic maroon beads and traditional crafts to mahogany and ebony furniture and plenty of fish. Local cuisine echoes much of what is found elsewhere in southern Africa: *nsima* (porridge), *rape* (the Malawian version of *morogo*), pumpkin leaves, sweet potatoes and the generous use of *nsijiro* (ground nut flour). Another favourite is *chinangwa*, a very filling, potato-like vegetable that is peeled, boiled in saltwater, sliced and served with tea instead of bread. Other favourites include okra, Chinese cabbage, *tarpis*, red-skinned potatoes and red onions. Because Malawi has the largest lake in Africa, fish features prominently on the local menu, and Malawians eat twice as much fish as meat. The most common fish varieties are *chambo* (the collective name of six species of tilapia), *kampango* (a larger, tasty fish) and *usipa* (a very small fish, often dried).

Chambo, a favourite that features prominently on hotel and restaurant menus, is prepared in many ways: curried, stewed, grilled whole, or dried. These fish are rather bony but extremely tasty.

MBATATA
Sweet Potato and Mince Bake

SERVES 4-6

60 ml (4 T) oil
2 large sweet potatoes, peeled and thinly sliced
1 bunch spring onions, chopped
500 g (18 oz) minced beef
4 tomatoes, peeled and chopped
1 tin (75 g/3 oz) tomato paste
15 ml (1 T) vinegar
salt and pepper to taste
breadcrumbs

CHEESE SAUCE:
30 ml (2 T) butter/margarine
15 ml (1 T) flour
250 ml (1 cup) milk
45 ml (3 T) grated cheese

Heat 45 ml (3 T) of the oil in a saucepan and fry the sweet potatoes until brown. Remove and keep warm.

In another saucepan, heat the remaining oil and fry the onions until they are soft. Add the mince and brown it. Add the tomatoes, tomato paste, vinegar and seasoning. Cover and simmer for 30 minutes.

Grease a large ovenproof dish. Arrange layers of sweet potatoes and mince stew in it.

CHEESE SAUCE: Melt butter/margarine in a saucepan, add the flour and cook for 1 minute, stirring continuously. Add the milk and stir until thickened. Remove from the heat and add the cheese.

Pour the sauce over the meat, sprinkle with breadcrumbs and bake at 180 °C (350 °F/gas 4) for 45 minutes.

STEWED NKWANI
Pumpkin Leaves

SERVES 4

1 bunch pumpkin leaves
water
2 ml (½ t) bicarbonate of soda
salt and pepper to taste
1 onion, chopped
2 tomatoes, chopped

Rinse the pumpkin leaves thoroughly under running water and remove the strings. Slice thinly and place in a saucepan.

Cover the leaves with water, add bicarbonate of soda (to help retain the colour of the leaves), salt and pepper.

Bring to the boil and then add the onion and tomatoes. Reduce the heat and simmer for about 20 minutes, or until cooked.

Okra (ladies' fingers) are readily available and very cheap in Malawi, especially during the rainy season. They are best used young, as they become fibrous and slimy when older. Okra can be cooked with lemon juice to eradicate any sliminess. When buying okra, the ends should snap off crisply.

KAPENTA YAIMPIKWA
Fresh Kapenta

SERVES 4

500 ml (2 cups) kapenta
125 ml (½ cup) oil
2 large onions, chopped
3 tomatoes, peeled and chopped
10 ml (2 t) salt
3 ml (½ t) Aromat

Clean the kapenta with hot water. Heat the oil in a pan and fry the fish for about 10 minutes until brown.

Add the onions and tomatoes to the kapenta and mix well. Simmer gently for 5 minutes.

Serve with porridge (for the Zambian equivalent of Malawi's *nsima,* see the recipe for *nshima* on page 86).

Kapenta is a tiny fish, popular in Zambia, Malawi and Zimbabwe. It is available fresh, but is mostly used in its dried form. This recipe can be used for both dry and fresh kapenta. If kapenta is not available, white-bait or any small white fish could be used instead.

MASAMBA CAKES
Spinach Cakes

MAKES 8

1 bunch *masamba* (spinach), rinsed
  and chopped
110 g (4 oz)/250 ml (1 cup) cooked macaroni
2 eggs
100 g (4 oz)/500 ml (2 cups) fresh breadcrumbs
salt to taste
2 ml (½ t) sugar
60 g (2 oz)/125 ml (½ cup) cake flour
60 g (2 oz)/60 ml (4 T) butter/margarine
water

Place the spinach in a saucepan and cook
until wilted. Chop finely.

Mix the macaroni into the spinach, add
1 egg, half the breadcrumbs, salt and sugar.

Mix well and form into flat cakes.

Beat the second egg and mix it with
the remaining breadcrumbs in a separate
container. Coat the cakes in flour and then in
the egg and breadcrumbs mixture.

Heat the oil and fry the cakes until cooked
through. Serve with a savoury sauce.

MANDAZI
Fat Cakes

MAKES 24

480 g (17 oz)/4 x 250 ml (4 cups) cake flour
30 ml (2 T) baking powder
10 ml (2 t) cream of tartar
100 g (4 oz)/125 ml (½ cup) sugar
4 eggs, beaten
± 250 ml (1 cup) milk to mix
oil for deep frying

Sift together the flour, baking powder and cream of tartar.

Add the sugar and carefully mix in the eggs.

Add enough milk to form a stiff batter.

Heat the oil, drop spoonfuls of batter into the hot oil and deep-fry until brown on all sides.

Drain on kitchen paper and serve hot with tea.

Variation:
Add 5 crushed cardamom seeds to the mixture before frying. Serve with a savoury mince filling or with jam.

STEWED CHAMBO

SERVES 6

30 ml (2 T) oil
2 onions, chopped
4 tomatoes, peeled and chopped
5 ml (1 t) turmeric
salt and pepper to taste
1 whole chambo of approximately 500 g (18 oz), or any other firm white fish, cut into portions

Heat the oil in a saucepan and sauté the onions until they are transparent.

Add the tomatoes, turmeric, salt and pepper.

Simmer until thickened.

Add the chambo pieces, adding some water if the stew seems dry.

Heat until boiling, cover the saucepan, reduce the heat and simmer for about 30 minutes, until the fish is cooked.

Variation:
Dried chambo is steamed and served topped with the same sauce as described above, or brushed with oil and grilled. One dried chambo serves 4.

ZANZIBAR

THE EXOTIC ISLAND OF ZANZIBAR off the East African coast has ancient links with both Arabia and the mainland of Africa. The Arab influence on Zanzibar and Pemba islands is reflected in the inhabitants, a mixture of Shirazis (from ancient Persia), Arabs and Comorans (from the Comoros islands).

Zanzibar was initially granted independence in 1963, when power passed to the ruling class of the Sultan and Arabs. Albeid Karume, leader of the Afro-Shiraz Party, took power in January 1964 after a violent revolution. He later became the first president of the Republic of Tanzania. Later that same year, Zanzibar finally became part of the United Republic of Tanzania – now the largest of the East African countries – when the newly independent territories of Tanganyika and Zanzibar merged into one nation.

Despite the union, however, Zanzibar remains somewhat isolated and separate. Although the Zanzibar people speak Swahili (kiswahili), they continue to embrace the Arab culture and Islamic faith. Zanzibar's food, therefore, incorporates a little Arabic cuisine, generous quantities of aromatic Indian spices, and a touch of Africa.

Zanzibar's prosperity was based largely on cloves and, for many years, it was the sole supplier of cloves until other countries started growing the popular spice. This forced Zanzibar to look to tourism to boost its revenue and the spice tour is very popular. It is facinating to see black pepper, nutmeg, turmeric and cloves in their raw state.

While visiting, the women taught me how to roll pastry for samoosas and *chapattis*, while other typical dishes included *Kaimati* (grated coconut fritters), cassava in coconut sauce, and *tambi* (noodles in syrup). Coconut milk is used in many recipes, and is made by breaking a fresh coconut open and shredding the flesh, which is then mixed with cold water and squeezed through a strainer.

CHICKEN WITH MANGO SAUCE

SERVES 6-8

1 whole chicken of 750 g-1 kg (1½ - 2½ lb)
750 ml (3 cups) water
salt to taste
2 garlic cloves, crushed
1 onion, chopped
3 ml (½ t) cinnamon
5 ml (1 t) black pepper
250 ml (1 cup) coconut milk
2 green mangoes, sliced

SAUCE:
250 ml (1 cup) coconut milk
45 ml (3 T) oil
250 ml (1 cup) mashed potatoes
salt and pepper to taste
10 ml (2 t) turmeric

GARNISH:
1 mango, sliced
1 onion, sliced
1 egg, hard-boiled and sliced
1 tomato, sliced

Cook the chicken in salted water with the garlic, onion, cinnamon, black pepper, coconut milk and green mangoes.

When the chicken has cooked through, remove the mango slices and prepare the sauce.

SAUCE: Boil together the coconut milk and oil. Add the mashed mango (from the chicken) and the mashed potatoes. Season with salt and pepper and turmeric. Moisten with stock from the cooked chicken.

TO SERVE: Place the chicken on a serving platter, pour the sauce over it and garnish with mango slices, sliced onion, sliced hard-boiled egg and sliced tomato.

LOBSTER MAYONNAISE

SERVES 1

1 lobster
250 ml (1 cup) water
juice of 1 lemon
salt and pepper to taste
1 onion, sliced
75 ml (5 T) mayonnaise
45 ml (3 T) water
freshly ground pepper to taste

Remove the flesh from the lobster. Heat the water to boiling point and add the lemon juice, salt, pepper, onion and lobster flesh. Simmer for 10 minutes.

Remove the lobster and keep warm. In the same water, boil the lobster shell for 5 minutes. Remove and rinse under cold running water.

Place the shell on a serving dish. Slice the lobster flesh and spoon it into the shell.

Mix the mayonnaise with 45 ml (3 T) water and spread it on the lobster. Sprinkle with black pepper before serving.

FRIED OCTOPUS

SERVES 4

500 g (18 oz) octopus
water
30 g (1 oz)/30 ml (2 T) butter
30 ml (2 T) lemon juice
1 onion, chopped
1 garlic clove, chopped
15 ml (1 T) chopped ginger
2 green chillies, chopped
5 ml (1 t) cumin seeds
5 ml (1 t) turmeric

Cover the octopus with water and boil it for 20 minutes. Remove the octopus from the pot.

Meanwhile, in a large frying pan, melt the butter and add all the remaining ingredients. Sauté for about 10 minutes.

Add the octopus and stir-fry for 8 minutes. Serve with salad.

CHAPATIS

MAKES 8-10

240 g (9 oz)/500 ml (2 cups) cake flour
125 ml (½ cup) lukewarm water
125 ml (½ cup) coconut oil
45 ml (3 T) vegetable fat
45 ml (3 T) oil

DOUGH: Mix the flour with the lukewarm water, coconut oil and vegetable fat. Knead together until it makes a smooth, pliable dough. Form into large balls and leave to rest for about 30 minutes.

Roll the dough out into a large circle. Stretch it out and make a large hole in centre. Tear the dough to form it into a long strip, and form the strip into tight circles. Cover and allow to rest. Rollout again until thin and flat. Shallow-fry the chapatis in hot oil on a griddle or heavy-based frying pan.

ZANZIBAR MIX

SERVES 6- 8

BHAJIYAS:
200 g (7 oz)/250 ml (1 cup) lentils
125 ml (½ cup) oil
salt to taste

SAUCE:
250 ml (1 cup) water
45 ml (3 T) flour
10 ml (2 t) turmeric
salt to taste
1 mango, peeled and diced

POTATOES:
2 potatoes
2 green bananas

CASSAVA CRISPS:
2 cassava
250 ml (1 cup) oil
salt to taste
10 ml (2 t) chilli powder

RED OR GREEN CHUTNEY:
12 red or green chillies
salt to taste
1 green mango, cut into pieces
1 lemon, cut into small pieces
30 ml (2 T) sugar

LENTILS:
200 g (7 oz)/250 ml (1 cup) lentils
500 ml (2 cups) water
salt to taste

GARNISH:
ground nuts

BHAJIYAS: Soak the lentils overnight, drain and purée until smooth. Form the lentil purée into balls and deep-fry in the oil. Season with salt.

SAUCE: Heat the water to boiling point. Mix the flour with a little cold water to form a paste. Add the turmeric, salt and flour paste to the saucepan. Add the raw mango pieces and mix through. Cook for 1 minute.

POTATOES: Boil the potatoes until cooked, then peel and cut into quarters. In another saucepan, boil the green bananas for 10 minutes. Slice the bananas and mix with the potatoes.

CASSAVA CRISPS: Peel the cassava and slice into sticks. Deep-fry in hot oil, season with salt and chilli powder.

RED OR GREEN CHUTNEY: Cut the chillies through the middle, remove the seeds and place the chillies in a liquidiser. Add salt, pieces of lemon and green mango.

LENTILS: Soak the lentils overnight in salted water and boil for about 20 minutes until soft. Drain if all the water has not been absorbed.

TO ASSEMBLE: Place the potatoes in a bowl. Add the lentils and the sauce. Mix everything together. Cut the *bhajiyas* in half and put them on top, with the coconut chutney and the red or green chutney. Add the cassava crisps. Sprinkle with ground nuts and serve hot with chutneys.

VARIATION: The cassava crisps can be replaced with potato crisps.

CASSAVA AND CHANGU WITH COCONUT SAUCE

SERVES 6-8

2 cassava, peeled and boiled
125 ml (½ cup) coconut milk
1 whole changu

Cook the cassava in the coconut milk for about 20 minutes until it is soft.

Place the fish on top of the cassava and gently cook for about 30 minutes.

KAIMATI

SERVES 4-6

500 g (18 oz)/4 x 250 ml (4 cups) cake flour
1 packet (10 g) instant yeast
250 ml (1 cup) lukewarm milk
30 g (1 oz)/30 ml (2 T) butter
250 ml (1 cup) coconut milk

SYRUP:
500 ml (2 cups) water
200 g (7 oz)/250 ml (1 cup) sugar
15 ml (1 T) ground cinnamon

Mix together the flour and yeast. Mix the milk with the butter, add to the flour and knead to mix. Gradually add the coconut milk. Mix until the dough is smooth and pliable. Leave in a warm place until double in size.

Heat the oil and form the dough into balls the size of golf balls and deep-fry.

SYRUP: Boil all the ingredients together.

Dip the kaimati into the syrup and allow to cool. Serve as dessert or with coffee and tea.

VIPOPOO

MAKES ± 24

120 g (4½ oz)/250 ml (1 cup) cake flour
62,5 ml (¼ cup) each water and coconut milk
45 ml (3 T) sugar
10 ml (2 t) ground cardamom

Mix together the flour and water well. Roll into balls the size of small marbles.

Boil together the coconut milk, sugar and ground cardamom.

Add the pastry balls to the coconut milk and cook for 5 minutes. Serve as dessert.

TAMBI

SERVES 6-8

500 g (18 oz) tambi
750 ml (3 cups) water
salt
75 ml (5 T) sugar
45 ml (3 T) oil
6 cardamom seeds, crushed

Cook the tambi in boiling salted water for about 10 minutes until soft. Drain.

Sprinkle the tambi with sugar and oil, season with cardamom, mix through and serve.

COOKING FROM **CAPE TO CAIRO**

KENYA

KENYA REMAINS, FOR MANY PEOPLE, the epitome of Africa, and nowhere is this image more evident than in the abundance of its wildlife, most notably in the famed Masai Mara National Reserve.

The capital city, Nairobi, is bustling, friendly and the heart of the relatively prosperous country. Mombasa, steeped in a rich Arab history, is the largest port on the coast of East Africa and serves many neighbouring states.

Prior to colonialism, there were no pre-existing kingdoms uniting the individual African societies. Although the Sultan of Zanzibar exercised some control over Arab-dominated cities along the coast, he had little influence over the indigenous people of the interior.

Kenya is home to almost every major language group of Africa, including the "click" language of the San and Khoi, but the official languages are Swahili (kiswahili) and English. With a population of nearly 30 million, the main indigenous groups comprise Kikuyu, Kamba, Luhya and Maasai.

My host family in Mombasa was Mama-Omodi and her daughters. They all enthusiastically showed me how to prepare family meals Mombasa-style.

The open-air kitchen teems with life and the smell of food cooking on the *jiko* (charcoal burner) is inviting. The daughters take turns to break and grate the coconut, which is then placed in a wet *kifumbu* (conical basket) and squeezed to produce coconut milk. The spices are ground in a pestle and mortar, and the tomatoes crushed. Great care is taken when cleaning and gutting fish, and also in chopping and peeling fresh vegetables.

I encountered an unusual method of cooking rice, unique to Mombasa. Rice is placed in a saucepan with water and covered with a newspaper. Hot coals are placed on a tray on top of the paper. The rice simmers under the hot coals and after cooking, the dry top coat is gently removed so that it comes off in one piece.

UGALI CAKE AND SUKUMA WIKI WITH ZEBRA AND TOMATO CONCASSE

SERVES 4

± 1 litre (4 cups) water
360 g (12 oz)/750 ml (3 cups) *ugali*
  (maize-meal)
30 g (1 oz)/30 ml (2 T) butter/margarine
200 g (7 oz) *sukuma wiki*
2 onions, finely chopped
1 garlic clove, crushed
salt and pepper to taste
30 ml (2 T) oil
500 g (18 oz) zebra steak, cut into
  serving portions
1 carrot, cut into strips
1 brinjal, cut into strips
½ x 410 g (14 oz) can tomato concasse
  or salsa

Boil the water in a saucepan and then add the maize-meal. Cook, stirring continuously, until the porridge is stiff.

Melt the butter/margarine and fry the *sukuma wiki*, onions and garlic for 3 minutes. Season to taste.

Heat the oil and pan-fry the zebra steaks. Remove the steaks from the pan.

Add 15 ml (1 T) oil to the pan and fry the brinjal and carrot strips.

Arrange the steaks on warm plate with the *ugali* and *sukuma wiki*. Garnish with concasse or salsa and top with fried strips of carrots and brinjal.

BEEF STEW

SERVES 4-6

30 ml (2 T) oil
500 g (18 oz) beef, cubed
6 tomatoes, grated
250 ml (1 cup) coconut milk
15 ml (1 T) chopped coriander (dhania)
1 chilli, chopped
salt to taste

Heat the oil in a saucepan and brown the beef.

Add the remaining ingredients and simmer for about 45 minutes, until the meat is cooked.

MATAHA
Pea, Corn and Potato Mash

SERVES 4-6

500 ml (2 cups) shelled garden peas
500 ml (2 cups) corn from the cob
5 potatoes
30 ml (2 T) oil
salt to taste

Cook vegetables separately. Mash potatoes. Heat oil and add all the ingredients. Add salt to taste.

Heat through and mix until all the ingredients are mashed together.

PILAU

SERVES 4-6

30 ml (2 T) oil
500 g (18 oz) beef, cubed
15 ml (1 T) mixed spices
250 ml (1 cup) beef stock
150 g (5 oz) peas
4 carrots, diced
200 g (7 oz)/250 ml (1 cup) uncooked rice

Heat the oil in a saucepan and brown the
beef with spices.

Add the stock the saucepan and cook
until the meat is tender.

Add the peas, carrots and rice, toss
together and cook for further 15 minutes.
Serve with *kachumbari* (tomato, onion and
vinegar salad).

Pilau is a popular dish at
weddings and other large
gatherings. Spices like
chillies, garlic, dhania, curry
powder and turmeric are
crushed together to produce
the desired flavour.

FISH STEW

SERVES 6-8

2 red onions, chopped
1 garlic clove, crushed
4 tomatoes, peeled and chopped
2 chillies, chopped
45 ml (3 T) ground coriander
15 ml (1 T) curry powder
5 ml (1 t) turmeric
250 ml (1 c) oil
1 whole tafi, cod or kabeljou
250 ml (1 c) tomato purée
1 can (75 g) tomato paste
250 ml (1 cup) coconut milk
15 ml (1 T) coriander (dhania) leaves

Place the onions, garlic and tomatoes in a blender and purée until smooth.

Mix the chillies, coriander, curry and turmeric, and grind the mixed spices. Cut deep slits into the fish and rub the fish with the mixed spices, pressing well into the slits.

Heat the oil and deep-fry the fish.

Remove the fish and place it in a saucepan. Add the tomato purée, tomato paste, coconut milk and chopped dhania leaves.

Bring to the boil and then simmer for about 10 minutes. Garnish with dhania leaves.

SKEWERED IRIO BALLS WITH BARRACUDA IN COCONUT SAUCE

SERVES 4

200 g (7 oz) potatoes, peeled
   and boiled
100 g (4 oz) frozen peas, cooked
200 g (7 oz) *sukuma wiki,* cooked
½ tin (410 g /14 oz) creamed
   sweet corn
salt and pepper to taste
125 ml (½ cup) flour
oil for frying
50 ml (3 T) oil
500 g (18 oz) barracuda
2 onions, chopped
1 garlic clove, crushed
30 ml (2 T) chopped coriander
   (dhania)
3 ml (½ t) turmeric
200 ml (1 cup) coconut milk

Mash the potatoes, peas, *sukuma wiki*, sweet corn and seasoning. Form into balls the size of golf balls, roll in flour and deep-fry in hot oil. Thread onto 4 skewers.

Heat 15 ml (1 T) oil and pan-fry fish. Remove from pan and keep warm. Add remaining oil top and sauté onions, garlic and dhania until soft.

Add the turmeric and coconut milk and cook for 3 minutes.

Place the skewered vegetables on a warm plate. Arrange the fried fish, pour sauce around the fish and serve immediately.

Traditionally, the fish is grilled on a *jigo* or charcoal burner. The grill is prepared by brushing it with oil, using the hairy peel of the coconut.

BRINJAL STEW

SERVES 4-6

4 brinjals, peeled
45 ml (3 T) oil
1 onion, sliced
10 ml (2 t) curry powder
250 ml (1 cup) coconut milk
salt

Slice the brinjals lengthways, but do not cut right through.

Heat the oil and fry the onion with the curry powder until soft.

Add the coconut milk and heat until it boils.

Add the brinjals, season and allow to simmer for about 20 minutes until cooked.

The brinjals in Kenya are long, narrow and green. Use the local variety if you cannot find them.

GRILLED CHANGU

SERVES 6-8

1 whole changu, cod or kabeljou
oil for basting
salt and pepper to taste

Grill the fish on both sides for 30 minutes, or until cooked. Serve with rice.

VARIATION: Grill the fish for 15 minutes only. Bring 250 ml (1 cup) coconut milk to the boil in a saucepan, add the grilled fish and cook for another 15 minutes.

MUSHICHA AND PEAS

SERVES 4

1 bunch of muchicha, washed and steamed
250 ml (1 cup) peas
4 tomatoes, grated
2 red onions, chopped
250 ml (1 cup) coconut milk

Rinse the muchicha and peas. Steam together until soft.

Add the tomatoes, onions, and coconut milk. Mix to blend.

Simmer gently for about 20 minutes until cooked through. Serve with porridge (see the recipe for *nshima* on page 86 for the Zambian equivalent of Kenya's *ugali*).

COOKING FROM
TO
CAPE
GHANA

AS EARLY AS THE THIRTEENTH CENTURY, a number of kingdoms were established in Ghana and each had a strong culture of trading. The best known and most powerful of these nations was the Ashanti kingdom, which by the late seventeenth century had conquered most of the other groups.

The Ashanti capital of Kumasi was highly efficient, with facilities and services equal to most European capitals at the time – but all this came to rather abrupt end with the beginning of the slave trade to the Americas in the 1800s.

The modern state of Ghana extends from the Gulf of Guinea and stretches approximately 640 km inland. Most of the countryside consists largely of wooded hills and wide valleys, with a low-lying coastal plain.

Ghana gained its independence from Britain in 1957, but many of its 18-million-strong population speak English, and it is the country's official language, with the main African languages Akan, Twi, Fante, Ga, Ewe, Dagbeni, Hausa and Nzima. Although most Ghanaians are Christian, many still follow traditional beliefs and there is a minority of Muslims.

The capital of Ghana is the lively Accra, and the vibrant lifestyle, colourfully dressed Ghanaians and buzzing city centre make Accra a truly African metropolis.

A lot of food is sold on the streets. Rice with spicy chicken or fish stew is wrapped artistically in banana leaves, and plantains – a type of banana – are roasted on open fires and sold by street vendors. Women, carrying large dishes of vegetables and fruit on their heads in true African style, walk up and down the streets, selling their wares.

Ghanaian food has a distinct flavour: most dishes are delicately spiced with chillies, garlic, palm oil and peanut sauce. I enjoyed the crumbly but moist *gari foto* and the "light soups" made with tilapia fish or goats' milk, which are served with the tangy *kenkey*, sticky *fufu*, or the robust *banku*.

GARI FOTO

SERVES 4-6

75 ml (5 T) soya oil
2 onions, sliced
15 ml (1 T) chilli pepper
4 tomatoes, chopped
30 ml (2 t) tomato paste
1 tin (175 g/6 oz) tuna, drained
2 carrots, diced
1 green pepper, chopped
4 eggs
30 ml (2 T) water
250 ml (1 cup) gari
lettuce leaves

Heat the oil, add the onions and chilli pepper and sauté until soft.

Add the tomatoes and tomato paste to the onions. Stew for 15 minutes.

Add the tuna, carrots, and green pepper and allow to simmer until soft.

Beat 3 eggs and boil 1 until hard. Slowly stir the beaten eggs into the sauce.

Sprinkle water lightly on gari and gently mix the sauce into the gari. Check the seasoning.

Garnish a serving platter with lettuce leaves and spoon the gari foto on the lettuce. Garnish with the boiled egg, cut into wedges.

Gari is made of dried and ground cassava. Replace it with cooked *phutu* (page 30) or maize-rice.

The *kapenta* or anchovies used in this recipe can be replaced with any small salted fish.

OKRA STEW WITH BANKU

SERVES 4

500 g (18 oz) fish or goat meat
250 ml (1 cup) water
1 onion, chopped
45 ml (3 T) palm oil
2 tomatoes, chopped
1 green or yellow pepper, chopped
100 g (4 oz) kapenta or anchovies
250 ml (1 cup) okra, chopped
1 brinjal, chopped
125 ml (½ cup) wele (optional)

Cook the fish or goat meat in a little water until tender – approximately 20 minutes in the case of fish, and 1 hour for goat.

Fry the onion in palm oil until soft. Add the chopped tomatoes, green or yellow pepper and kapenta or anchovies. Simmer for 5 minutes. Add the okra and brinjal.

Mix in the cooked fish or meat and bring to the boil. If preferred, add wele (cow skin) for added flavour. Cook until the fish or meat is soft.

KENKEY

SERVES 6

500 ml (2 cups) raw maize kernels
water
salt to taste
banana leaves

Cover the maize with water and soak for
three days. Rinse the maize and pound it to
a pulp or blend until smooth.

Bind with a little water to for a thick dough.
Allow to stand for another day to ferment.

Divide the dough into three parts. Cook two
parts, softened with water, in a heavy pot for
30 minutes, stirring. Remove from the heat
and mix with rest of the raw dough. Add salt.

Mould the *kenkey* into tennis ball shapes
and wrap tightly with enough banana leaves
to cover them completely. Line the pot with
banana leaves and place the *kenkey* balls
on the leaves.

Top with water and cook for 3 hours. Serve
with meat or fish.

CHARCOAL-GRILLED RED SNAPPER

SERVES 4

1 whole snapper, approximately 500 g (18 oz)
15 ml (1 T) chilli powder
15 ml (1 T) crushed ginger
1 garlic clove, crushed
3 tomatoes, chopped
1 onion, chopped
1 green sweet pepper, chopped
salt to taste

OIL FOR BASTING:
45 ml (3 T) soya oil
15 ml (1 T) each crushed garlic and ginger
1 bay leaf
3 ml (½ t) aniseed
salt to taste

SAUCE: Blend the chilli, ginger and garlic with
a little of the chopped tomatoes and onions
and use this as the base for the sauce.

OIL FOR BASTING: Blend all the ingredients.

Score the fish on both sides and baste it
with the oil mixture. Grill for 20 minutes.

Pour the blended chilli mixture on a serving
platter. Top with the grilled fish.

Mix remaining onion and tomato with green
pepper, and spread the mixture on top of
the fish. Serve with *kenkey*.

TILAPIA LIGHT SOUP AND BANKU

SERVES 4-6

1 whole tilapia
1 large onion, chopped
2 large tomatoes, chopped
1 yellow pepper, chopped
1 brinjal, peeled and chopped
45 ml (3 T) palm oil
500 ml (2 cups) chicken stock

Scale and gut the tilapia.

Make a stew by frying the onion, tomatoes, yellow pepper and brinjal in the palm oil until the vegetables are soft.

Add the chicken stock and tilapia.

Cook gently for about 20 minutes until the fish is cooked through and flaky.

If tilapia is not available, it can be replaced with any firm-fleshed white fish. *Banku* is a type of dumpling made with cassava flour (*gari*) or corn meal, and steamed in the stew. The preparation method is similar to that of wholewheat dumplings (see the recipe for *idombolo* on page 53).

COCONUT OR PEANUT BISCUITS

MAKES 12

250 ml (1 cup) sugar
300 g (10 oz)/750 ml (3 cups)
  peanuts **or**
240 g (9 oz)/750 ml (3 cups)
  desiccated coconut
15 ml butter/margerine
30 ml (2 T) glucose syrup
60 ml (4 T) water

Caramellise the sugar by heating it over a low heat until it has melted.

Add the peanuts or coconut and stir to blend.

Rub a table top or chopping board with butter and pour the mixture on to it. Add glucose syrup and water and mix well.

Roll the mixture out with a rolling pin and cut into attractive shapes. Leave to dry and serve as dessert.

SENEGAL NESTLES COMFORTABLY IN THE WESTERN EXTREME OF THE AFRICAN CONTINENT, bound by Mauritania to the north, Mali to the east, Guinea and Guinea-Bissau to the south – and the Atlantic Ocean to the west.

Senegal was an early participant in the slave trade. Ile de Goree – 16 hectares of arid land less that 10 kilometres from the mainland and one of the first French settlements in Africa – still bears evidence of the horrors of this trade. The capital, Dakar, is a large modern city, and a major West African port, home to about an eighth of Senegal's population of 8.5 million. Although the country has around 20 ethnic groups, including the Wolofs, Fulani and the Serer, the people of Senegal enjoy a harmonious relationship, intermarrying freely.

Senegal gained independence from France in 1974, but French remains the official language. Artistic expression is rich and varied, but Senegal is best known for its musicians and, perhaps most significantly, the drum, a key element of local music.

Thiebou djeun, pronounced "cheebo-oo-jenn", is the country's national dish, and Senegalese all over the world make a point of preparing this dish to remind them of home. The ingredients are easily accessible: *thiebou djeun* can range from a simple bowl of rice and vegetables to more exotic additions like fish. To honour guests, the Senegalese will serve *poulet yassa*, a lemon-marinated onion and chicken dish.

As in most of Africa, peanuts play an important role in local food. *Mafe* is a peanut sauce-based stew made with chicken, beef or mutton, and considered one of Senegal's culinary pillars. Traditionally, food is cooked on charcoal burners to ensure that it cooks slowly and that the flavours blend to perfection. After a meal, a sweet, minty green tea is served as a digestive. It is also an art unto itself to pour this tea. The tiny tea pot is held high and the steaming hot tea gently falls in to the tiny glasses in which it is served.

POULET YASSA
Chicken in Onion Sauce

SERVES 4-6

4 onions, sliced
125 ml (½ cup) lemon juice
salt and black pepper to taste
3 ml (½ t) cayenne pepper
45 ml (3 T) oil
1 large chicken, cut into portions
45 ml (3 T) mustard

Mix together the onions, lemon juice and
seasoning. Leave to stand for 30 minutes.

Heat the oil and fry the onions gently until
transparent.

Meanwhile, coat the chicken pieces with
mustard, salt and pepper. Marinate 15 minutes.

Deep-fry or oven-roast the chicken portions
until brown and cooked through.

Add the chicken to the onion sauce. Cook
gently to blend the flavours, the longer the
better. Moisten with water if it gets dry. Serve
hot on cooked rice.

MAFFÉ DíAGREOU
Lamb with Peanut and Okra sauce

SERVES 4-6

45 ml (3 T) oil
500 g (18 oz) lamb, cut into cubes
2 onions, chopped
2 tomatoes, peeled and chopped
75 g (5 T) tomato paste
100 g (4 oz) peanut butter
2 sweet potatoes, peeled and quartered
100 g (3 oz) fresh okra, trimmed and chopped
1 large cassava, peeled and chopped
1 red sweet pepper, chopped
salt and pepper to taste
500 ml (2 cups) water

Heat the oil and brown the lamb. Remove
it from the pot and keep it warm.

Add the onions to the pot and sauté
until transparent. Add all the remaining
ingredients, except the water, and stir-fry
for about 5 minutes.

Add the water, return the lamb to the
pot and simmer, covered, for about
50-60 minutes. Serve on rice.

THIOF FARCI Á LA SAINT LOUISIEN
Stuffed Fish in Vegetable Stew

SERVES 6-8

1 whole thiof of approximately 500 g (18 oz)

STUFFING:
500 g (18 oz) fish steaks, filleted
500 ml (2 cups) breadcrumbs

SAUCE:
45 ml (3 T) peanut oil
1 onion, chopped
1 garlic clove, crushed
1 red sweet pepper, seeded and chopped
1 bouquet garni (2-3 sprigs of parsley,
    1 sprig of thyme and 1-2 bay leaves)
1 tin (115 g/4 oz) tomato paste
4 ripe tomatoes, pulped
500 ml (2 cups) water

VEGETABLES:
1 carrot, peeled and coarsely chopped
1 leek, coarsely chopped
1 red sweet pepper, seeded and cut into
    large pieces
100 g (4 oz) cabbage, cut into large pieces
1 brinjal, quartered
3 potatoes, peeled and quartered
salt and pepper to taste

**Thiof may be substituted
with any firm white fish.**

Preheat the oven to 180 °C (350 °F/gas 4).

Clean and cut the fish.

STUFFING: Purée the fish steaks and breadcrumbs in a blender.

Stuff the fish and place it in a large oven dish.

SAUCE: Heat the oil and sauté the onion, garlic and red pepper until soft. Add the bouquet garni, tomato paste, tomatoes and water.

Pour the sauce over the fish. Place all the prepared vegetables around the fish.

Cover and bake at for 45 minutes. Serve with rice.

THIEBOU DJEUN
Fish Stew with Mixed Vegetables

SERVES 6-8

1 kg (2½ lb) whole thiof, or any firm-fleshed
  white fish
1 onion, grated
1 garlic clove, crushed
30 ml (2 T) chopped parsley
2 chillies, chopped
60 ml (4 T) oil
125 ml (½ cup) tomato purée
4 tomatoes, peeled and chopped
½ cabbage, cut into large chunks
4 carrots, peeled and cut in half
2 brinjals, quartered
4 x 250 ml (4 cups) water
salt and pepper to taste
500 ml (2 cups) rice

Cut deep slits in the fish. Mix the onion,
garlic, parsley and chillies to a paste. Rub
this paste into the slits. Allow to stand for at
least 1 hour.

Cut the fish into big chunks. Heat the oil
and deep-fry the fish until brown.

Place the tomato purée, tomatoes,
vegetables and water in a saucepan and
cook until soft. Season with salt and pepper.
Add the fish to the vegetable stew and cook
for 10 minutes.

Remove fish and vegetables with a
slotted spoon and keep warm in oven. Use
the sauce to cook the rice, adding more
water if necessaryw. Check the seasoning.
Cook the rice about 30 minutes.

Spread the rice on a large platter. Arrange
the fish and vegetables on top.

ṢOUPIKANDIA RIZ À LA SAUCE GOMBO
Seafood and Okra Stew on Rice

SERVES 4

125 ml (½ cup) palm oil
1 onion, chopped
500 g (18 oz) white fish, filleted and diced
250 g (9 oz) fresh okra, trimmed and chopped
2 red sweet peppers, chopped
50 g (2 oz) dried fish, finely chopped
salt and pepper to taste
10 ml (2 t) chopped parsley
250 g (9 oz) shrimps or oysters (optional)
500 ml (2 cups) water

Heat the oil, add the chopped onion and
sauté until transparent.

Add all the remaining ingredients. Simmer
gently for 45 minutes until the fish is cooked
through and the vegetables are soft.

Garnish with cooked whole okra and pepper.
Serve with rice.

Thiebou djeun is Senegal's
national dish. Local fish, such
as maruo or thiof, is used and it
is served on short-grain rice.

PASTELLE

MAKES ±12

DOUGH:
120 g (4½ oz)/250 ml (1 cup) flour
salt to taste
1 egg, beaten
water
15 ml (1 T) oil

FILLING:
1 onion, grated
30 ml (2 T) chopped parsley
1 garlic clove, crushed
250 ml (1 cup) cooked white fish
salt and pepper to taste

Mix together the flour, salt, egg and enough water to form a stiff dough. Pour the oil over the dough and leave to soak for 30 minutes.

Knead the dough again, incorporating the oil. Roll out thinly and cut first into strips and then into squares.

FILLING: Combine all the ingredients and purée in a blender until smooth.

Place a teaspoon of filling on each pastry square, seal tightly and deep-fry in hot oil.

MOROCCO IS INDEED A LAND OF CONTRASTS.
Moulded by its many different people and
demarcated by stark geographical features,
such as the Rif and Atlas mountains that form
its backbone, the country borders both the
Atlantic and Mediterranean coasts, proudly
occupying the northwest corner of Africa.

Its cities, such as Casablanca, Marrakesh,
Fes and the capital at Rabat, teem with life
and people, ranging from the traditional
Berber-speaking mountain peasants to the
urbane, French-speaking upper echelons.

The French and Spanish restored Morocco's
independence in 1956 and, as one of Africa's
three monarchies, the country has since been
ruled by Muhammed V and his son Hassan II.

The majority of Morocco's population of
nearly 28 million are Sunni Muslims, and the
official languages are Arabic, French, Spanish
and English.

North African food – exotic, colourful and rich
with flavours of warm spices – has become
increasingly popular throughout the
world. The staple grain, couscous,
is always accompanied by spicy stews
called *tajines*, aromatic chicken, lamb
or beef dishes generously flavoured with
saffron and olives. Moroccan mezes are
mostly purées, dips, marinated olives and
cooked or raw vegetables.

Characteristic of Moroccan cuisine are the
pastries made from wafer-thin *warka*, rich
desserts and the popular mint tea, which
locals fondly refer to as "Moroccan whisky".
The succession of different peoples who have
invaded, traded with or visited North Africa
over the centuries have all left their culinary
legacies. The diet of the nomadic Berbers
and Bedouins is still evident today: *smen*
(a cooked and aged butter), dates and grains
(such as couscous) may be attributed to
these groups. The Mediterranean influence is,
of course, also apparent in the mezes served
as the first course.

BíSTILLA
Chicken or Pigeon Pie

SERVES 8

1 medium chicken, jointed, or 2 young pigeons
2 onions, grated
3 ml (½ t) saffron
3 ml (½ t) ginger
3 ml (½ t) ground cinnamon
90 ml (6 T) oil
salt and pepper to taste
1 bunch fresh coriander (dhania), chopped
1 bunch fresh parsley, chopped
8 eggs, beaten
10 sheets phyllo pastry
100 g (4 oz)/250 ml (1 cup) blanched almonds,
   coarsely chopped and toasted
20 ml (4 t) ground cinnamon for sprinkling
   (optional)
60 ml (4 T) icing sugar for sprinkling (optional)

Put the chicken or pigeons in a large saucepan. Add the onions, ginger, saffron, cinnamon, 45 ml (3 T) of the oil and seasoning. Add a little water – the meat should braise, not boil. Cover and cook gently, turning occasionally until tender.

Remove the meat and leave to cool. Discard the skin and bones. Add the coriander and parsley to the pan and boil, uncovered, until reduced to a thick sauce.

Over a low heat, gently stir in the eggs and scramble them. Remove from heat.

Pre-heat the oven to 190 °C (375 °F/gas 5). Thoroughly oil a 32 x 5 cm (13 x 2 in) baking tin. Lay a sheet of phyllo pastry in the tin, allowing the loose edges to fall over the sides. Brush with oil. Repeat layers four times, covering the tin completely.

Cover with the chicken or pigeon pieces, then the egg mixture. Cover with a small sheet of phyllo pastry and scatter over the almonds. Sprinkle with 10 ml (2 t) cinnamon and 30 ml (2 T) of the icing sugar, if preferred.

Fold the overhanging edges of the pastry over the almonds. Cover with the remaining pastry, brushing each sheet with oil. Tuck the edges inside the tin and under the pie.

Bake for about 45 minutes until crisp and golden. If preferred, sieve 30 ml (2 T) icing sugar over the top and make a lattice pattern with the remaining 10 ml (2 t) ground cinnamon. Serve hot with a salad.

Bístilla is one of the great dishes of North Africa. It is served hot as a first course, and is best eaten using the fingers. In Morocco, the crust is made of tissue-thin *warka*, for which phyllo pastry is the most practical substitute.

BEEF TAJINE WITH PRUNES

SERVES 6-8

45 ml (3 T) olive or sunflower oil
1 large onion, chopped
2 garlic cloves, crushed
1 kg (2½ lb) stewing beef, cut into large
  portions
50 ml (3 T) chopped parsley
5 ml (1 t) ground cinnamon
5 ml (1 t) ground cumin
3 ml (½ t) ground ginger
10 ml (2 t) freshly ground black pepper
3 ml (½ t) saffron or 5 ml (1 t) turmeric
375 ml (1½ cups) water
750 g (9 oz) prunes, halved and stoned
15 ml (1 T) clear honey
salt to taste
toasted sesame seeds
chopped almonds

In a large saucepan, heat the oil and stir in the onion, garlic, beef, parsley and spices. Cook until the meat is browned all over.

Stir in the water and simmer, covered for about 1½ hours until the meat is tender.

Add the prunes, honey and salt. Cover again and simmer for a further 30 minutes.

Serve on couscous (see recipe on page 130) and garnish with sesame seeds and almonds.

TAJINE DE POULET MQUALLI
Chicken Tajine with Olives and Preserved Lemons

SERVES 4

45 ml (3 T) olive oil
1 onion, chopped
3 garlic cloves, crushed
salt and pepper to taste
3 ml (½ t) ground ginger
8 ml (1½ t) ground cinnamon
large pinch of saffron threads or
3 ml (½ t) ground saffron
1,5 kg (3½ lb) chicken
700 ml (2½ cups) chicken stock or water
100 g (4 oz)/125 ml (½ cup) green-brown
   Moroccan olives, drained, or green and black
   olives, drained
1 preserved lemon, peeled, rinsed and chopped
1 bunch coriander (dhania), finely chopped

Heat the oil and fry the onion until golden.
Stir the garlic, salt, pepper, ginger, cinnamon
and saffron into the onions and cook until
fragrant, then spread over the chicken.

Place chicken in a heavy saucepan. Add the
stock or water and heat until boiling. Reduce
the heat, cover and simmer for 1½ hours,
turning the chicken 2 to 3 times.

Add the olives, preserved lemon and
herbs. Cover again and cook for 15 minutes.
Check the seasoning, transfer the chicken
to a serving dish and keep warm. Cut into
portions if preferred.

Reduce the cooking juices to a rich sauce,
skim off excess fat and pour the sauce over
the chicken. Serve with couscous.

COUSCOUS

SERVES 6-8

500 g (18 oz) couscous
60 ml (4 T) *smen/ghee* or melted butter
250 ml (1 cup) boiling water

Rub the *smen/ghee* or melted butter into the
couscous (this helps to separate the grains).

Pour over the boiling water, stir well and
leave for 10 minutes. Fork through the
couscous to make sure the grains separate.

Put into a steamer or colander over a pot of
gently cooking meat or vegetables and cook
uncovered for 20 minutes.

Fork through the couscous again to
separate the grains, turn on to a warm
serving dish, dot with butter, and form into
a mound with a large well in the centre into
which to ladle the meat and/or vegetables.

PRESERVED LEMONS

30 ml (2 T) coarse salt
12 plump juicy lemons, preferably thin-skinned

Put 10 ml (2 t) coarse salt in a preserving jar.

Using a sharp knife and working on a plate, slice the lemons lengthways but not right through – leave the pieces joined at the bottom.

Remove any pips, pack 15 ml (1 T) coarse salt into the cuts, close the lemons and pack them into the jar. Pack the jar tightly.

Squeeze another lemon, pour the juice over the fruit, sprinkle with the remaining coarse salt and top up with boiling water to cover the fruit.

Preserved lemons play a major role in Moroccan cooking, and make a novel addition to non-Moroccan dishes. Thin-skinned lemons will yield the most juice. Once the jar has been opened, pour in a little olive oil to cover the surface and the lemons will keep for up to a year.

Close the jar tightly and keep in a warm place for 3 to 4 weeks. A white film might appear on top of the lemons — this is normal and harmless.

VARIATION: This also works well with limes. If preferred, 1 stick cinnamon, 3 whole cloves, 6 crushed coriander seeds, 3 black peppercorns and 1 bay leaf can be layered with the lemons.

HUMMOUS

SERVES 4-6

250 ml (1 cup) chickpeas
water
250 g (9 oz) sesame seeds
1 garlic clove, crushed
lemon juice to taste
15 ml (1 T) olive oil
salt

Soak the chickpeas overnight in water. Drain.

Put fresh water into a saucepan, add the chickpeas and cook until almost tender. Drain. Add sesame seeds and garlic.

Blend into a thick purée, adding a little cooking water if needed. Add lemon juice, salt and pepper to taste.

TO SERVE: Place the hummous in a bowl, make a hollow in the middle and pour in a little olive oil.

BABAGHANUSH

SERVES 4-6

1 kg (2½ lb) brinjals
30 ml (2 T) lemon juice
125 ml (½ cup) sesame oil
125 ml (½ cup) yoghurt
30 ml (2 T) chopped parsley
1 garlic clove, crushed
30 ml (2 T) olive oil
½ cucumber to garnish
salt and black pepper

Bake or roast the brinjals in their skin at 180 °C (350 °F/gas 4) for about 1 hour until they are soft, and immerse immediately in cold water with lemon juice to preserve the colour. Cool, then peel, drain the juice and mash until smooth.

Add the rest of the ingredients and mix well. Place the mixture in a ceramic dish and garnish with cucumber slices.

TABOULEH

SERVES 4-6

250 ml (1 cup) finely ground bulgur (cracked wheat)
125 ml (½ cup) parsley, finely chopped
125 ml (½ cup) mint leaves, finely chopped
2 firm tomatoes, peeled and chopped
4 spring onions, finely chopped
salt and pepper
5 ml (1 t) *soemak* (Arabic spice)
45 ml (3 T) olive oil
45 ml (3 T) lemon juice

Soak the bulgur in water for 2 to 3 hours. Drain well.

Mix the parsley and mint with the tomatoes and onions.

Mix remaining ingredients. Pour over salad and toss well. Serve as part of the mezes.

Desserts are not common in African cuisine. Pastilla, with a milky sauce, is one of the few pastry desserts served in Morocco.

PASTILLA WITH MILK

SERVES 6-8

500 ml (2 cups) milk
30 ml (2 T) cornflour
30 ml (2 T) sugar
5-6 sheets phyllo pastry
250 ml (1 cup) chopped mixed nuts

Pre-heat the oven to 180 °C (350 °F/gas 4). Combine the milk, cornflour and sugar. Heat until boiling, reduce the heat and simmer, stirring until thickened.

Cut the phyllo pastry into large circles. Place alternate layers of phyllo pastry sheets and milk sauce on a round baking tray, top with nuts and bake for 20 minutes until golden.

Because gari is a little coarse, the eba will be a little coarse, but if done properly it should not be lumpy.

KOSAIN DOYA
Fried Grated Yam

MAKES 12

½ medium sized yam, peeled
1 large onion, grated
10 ml (2 t) black pepper
1 small tomato, diced
15 ml (1 T) flour
1 egg, beaten
salt and dried thyme to taste
oil for deep frying

Grate the yam into a bowl and add the rest of the ingredients, excluding the oil.

Heat oil in a frying pan, shape yam mixture into small balls or drop tablespoons-full of mixture into hot oil. Fry on both sides until golden brown and crisp, about 5-7 minutes.

Serve hot as a snack.

EBA

SERVES 4

1 litre (4 cups) water
750 ml (3 cups) gari

Bring water to a boil, lower the heat and add the gari, stirring consistently until the mixture has thickened.

Serve warm.

ETHIOPIA IS SAID TO BE THE CRADLE OF African
cuisine. It is called the land of thirteen months
of sunshine – the Ethiopian calendar has
twelve months of thirty days and an extra
month of five days called Pegume. Located
in the northeastern horn of the continent,
Ethiopia enjoys a partly pleasant and balmy
climate with rain falling rarely, except in the
summer months.

The fascinating thing about Ethiopia is
that primitive and modern cultures exist
side by side. In the villages, families live in
tukels made of stone with thatched roofs.
Life goes on today much as it has for
centuries. In Addis Ababa, the country's
capital, you will find new white buildings of
reinforced concrete in the midst of bustling,
energetic people.

The open-air market of Addis Ababa is the
largest and most exciting in all of Africa. The
markets stretch for miles with everything on
display – from clothing to household wares
and, of course, lots of food! The low stands
are heaped with all sorts of exotic fruits –
citrus fruits, bananas, grapes, pomegranates,
figs, custard apples (a delectable tropical

fruit), and a bounty of vegetables, including
the wonderful red onion of this area and
gommen, a kale-like plant. Meat such as beef,
lamb and goat are also on display. And you'll
find a sort of rancid butter, cut from a large
block and sold in chunks, wrapped in wax
paper, along with *lab*, a soft cheese wrapped
and kept cool in banana leaves.

A meal in Ethiopia is an experience. When
you have dinner in an Ethiopian home or
restaurant, you also eat the tablecloth! It is
the *injera*, the staple bread of Ethiopia, a
pancake-like bread made with sourdough.
It gets covered with an assortment of stews
and relishes, and as you eat, you tear off
a piece and use it to roll the food.

The hottest, most peppery food in all of
Africa is to be found in Ethiopia. *Beri-beri*
or *awaze* prepared with red pepper that has
been mixed with as many as fifteen spices,
is the country's favourite seasoning.

DORO AND SHIRO WAT
Chicken and Vegetable Stew

SERVES 4-6

1 chicken, cut into portions
65 ml (¼ cup) lemon juice
5 ml (1 t) salt
45 ml (3 T) butter
2 onions, finely chopped
1 clove garlic, crushed
15 cm piece of ginger, grated
45 ml (3 T) berbere spice
1 can (115 g/4 oz) tomato paste
65 ml (¼ cup) dry white wine
180 ml (¾ cup) water
1 can (410 g/14 oz) mixed vegetables
6 hard-boiled eggs, shelled

Rub chicken pieces with lemon juice and salt, and pierce all over with a fork. Allow to stand for 30 minutes.

Melt butter and cook onions until transparent. Add garlic, ginger, berbere and tomato paste and stir over low heat for 5 minutes.

Pour in wine and water. Bring to the boil, then reduce heat and simmer gently for 5 minutes, until liquid is reduced.

Pat chicken dry and place in simmering sauce, turning until well coated. Add the mixed vegetables. Reduce heat further, cover and simmer for 15 minutes.

Gently stir in eggs, cover and cook for a further 15 minutes.

Serve on a large platter with *injera* bread (see page 154).

SEGA WAT
Cubed Lamb

Prepare as with chicken stew (left) but use 1 kg of lamb (from leg) instead of chicken and only 1 cup of chopped onions. The lamb is cut in 10 cm cubes, the water is not added, and the lamb is sautéed on all sides until quite dry and well done.

ATERKEK ALECHA
Vegetable Stew

SERVES 4

250 ml (1 cup) vegetable oil (used as ¼ cup
   and ¾ cup)
2 large red onions, chopped
500 ml (2 cups) yellow split peas
5 ml (1 t) salt
3 ml (½ t) ground ginger
2 ml (¼ t) turmeric
750 ml (3 cups) water

Pour ¼ cup oil into a large pot and place over medium heat. Add onions and cook, stirring often, until the onions are golden brown. Add ¾ cup oil and add all other ingredients.

Cook over medium heat until the vegetables are tender.

Serve with *injera* (see page 154) made with vegetable oil instead of butter.

INJERA
Ethiopian Bread

SERVES 6-8

This unleavened bread of Ethiopia is really a huge pancake made by the women in special large pans with heavy covers. The *tef* batter is saved from an earlier baking and added to the new batter to give it a sourdough quality. It is poured at a thin consistency and baked covered so that the bottom of the pancake does not brown. The top should be full of air holes before the pancake is covered. The heavy cover steams the pancake so that when it is finished it looks like a huge thin rubber sponge. Since *tef* is not available here, we had to find a way to simulate *injera* in our test kitchen. The combination of buckwheat flour and biscuit mix seems to produce the closest substitute. Making it is easy, but getting the *injera* texture takes a bit of experimentation; first, because not all pancake mixes are alike and secondly, it is important to cook the pancake at just the right temperature. This takes a bit of practice.

250 ml (1 cup) ready-made pancake mix
190 ml (¾ cup) cake flour
3 ml (½ t) salt
15 ml (1 T) baking powder
250 ml (1 cup) soda water
1 beaten egg
30 ml (2 T) butter

Mix pancake mix, flour, salt and baking powder together in a medium bowl.

Add egg and soda and stir with a wooden spoon to combine.

Melt about 1 tablespoon of the butter in a skillet until bubbly. Pour in about 2 tablespoons of batter and cook for 2 minutes on each side until the bread is golden brown on both sides.

Remove the bread from the pan carefully to a plate.

Repeat, stacking the finished loaves on the plate to cool.

BERBERE
Spice Paste

MAKES 500 ML

5 ml (1 t) ground ginger
3 ml (½ t) ground cardamom
3 ml (½ t) ground coriander
3 ml (½ t) fenugreek seeds
2 ml (¼ t) ground nutmeg
2 ml (¼ t) ground cloves
2 ml (¼ t) ground cinnamon
2 ml (¼ t) ground allspice
1 small onion, grated
15 ml (1 T) finely chopped garlic
30 ml (2 T) salt
45 ml (3 T) red wine vinegar
50 ml paprika
30 ml (1 to 2 T) red pepper flakes (use larger
   quantity to make a hotter paste)
3 ml (½ t) black pepper
325 ml (1½ cups) water
30 ml (2 T) vegetable oil

Place ginger, cardamom, coriander, fenugreek seeds, nutmeg, cloves, cinnamon and allspice into a large frying pan. Toast the spices over medium-high heat for 1 minute, shaking the pan or stirring with a wooden spoon constantly. Let cool for 10 minutes. Put the spices, onion, garlic, salt, and vinegar in a blender and mix at high speed until the spices form a paste.

Toast the paprika, red pepper flakes and black pepper in a large frying pan for 1 minute, stirring constantly. Add water slowly to the pan, and then add the vegetable oil. Put the blender mixture into the pan, cook everything together for 15 minutes stirring constantly.

Place the paste in a jar and refrigerate.

NITER KEBBEH OR KIBE
Spiced Butter

MAKES 1 KG

900 g (2 lb) salted butter
20 ml (4 t) fresh ginger, finely grated
8 ml (1½ t) turmeric
2 ml (¼ t) cardamom seeds
1 stick of cinnamon
2 ml (¼ t) nutmeg
3 whole cloves
1 small yellow onion, peeled and
   coarsely chopped
45 ml (3 T) garlic, peeled and finely chopped

Melt the butter in a heavy saucepan over moderate heat, bringing the butter up to a light boil. When the surface is covered with white foam, stir in the remaining ingredients, including the onion and garlic. Reduce the heat to low and cook uncovered for about 45 minutes. Do not stir again.

Milk solids will form in the bottom of the pan and they should cook until they are golden brown. The butter will be clear.

Strain the mixture through several layers of cheesecloth placed in a strainer. Discard the milk solids left in the cheesecloth. Serve on toast, crackers, or use in cooking.

Store the spiced butter in a jar, covered, in the refrigerator (where it can keep up to 3 months).

LAB
Ethiopian Cheese

SERVES 4-6

500 g (18 oz) cottage cheese
60 ml (4 t) plain yogurt
15 ml (1 t) lemon rind, grated
30 ml (2 T) parsley, chopped
5 ml (1 t) salt
2 ml (¼ t) black pepper

Combine all the ingredients in a bowl. The mixture should be moist enough to spoon but dry enough to stay firm when served.

Place a clean piece of cheesecloth (or a very clean dishtowel) in a colander and pour mixture into the colander to drain off extra liquid. Gather the cheesecloth to make a sack and tie it with clean string or thread. Suspend from the faucet over the sink. (Another option is to tie the string to the handle of a door and to suspend the sack over a bowl.)

Allow to drain for several hours until the mixture has the consistency of soft cream cheese.

Serve with crackers or *injera*.

KITFO
Spiced Raw Beef

SERVES 6

65 ml (¼ cup) niter kebbeh (see recipe on p. 155)
1 small onion, finely chopped
¼ green sweet pepper, finely chopped
15 ml (1 T) chilli powder
3 ml (½ t) ginger, ground
2 ml (¼ t) finely chopped garlic
2 ml (¼ tsp) ground cardamom
3 ml (½ t) lemon juice
5 ml (1 t) berbere (see recipe on p. 155)
5 ml (1 t) salt
500g (18 oz) minced beef

Melt the niter kebbeh in a large frying pan. Add the onion, green pepper, chilli powder, ginger, garlic and cardamom. Cook for 2 minutes while stirring. Allow to cool for 15 minutes.

Add lemon juice, berbere, and salt. Stir in raw beef and serve.

COLLARD GREENS WITH MINCE OVER MACARONI

SERVES 4

450 g (16 oz) collard greens
60 ml (4 T) olive oil
2 small red onions, finely chopped
1 clove garlic, crushed
3 ml (½ t) grated fresh root ginger
500 g (18 oz) minced beef
2 green chillies, seeded and sliced
125 ml (½ cup) vegetable stock or water
salt and freshly ground pepper
1 can (410 g/14 oz) peas
1 red sweet pepper, seeded
  and sliced
250 ml (1 cup) macaroni

Wash collard greens, strip the leaves from the stalks and steam over a pan of boiling water for 5 minutes until lightly wilted. Set aside to cool and press out the excess water. Slice very thinly.

Heat the oil in a saucepan and fry the onions, garlic and ginger until transparent.

Add mince and stir-fry for a few minutes, then add the chillies and stock or water and seasoning. Cook for 20 minutes.

Add collard greens, peas with liquid, red pepper, salt and pepperand mix well. Cover and simmer over a low heat for about 15 minutes.

Cook pasta according to directions on packet. Serve collard greens with mince over macaroni.

The metropolis of the universe, the garden of the world, the anthill of the human species, the throne of royalty, a city embellished with castles and palaces, its horizon decorated with monasteries and with schools, and lit by the moons and stars of education. So said one bin Khaldun, a great medieval Arab historian, about Cairo.

Cairo, also dubbed the "Mother of the World", is said to be the largest city in Africa, and has a long and rich history. This last outpost of the African continent also completes the journey through Africa, from the Cape to Cairo.

Egypt lies on the north eastern point of Africa, stretching to the Mount Sinai region across the Suez Canal. The great Nile River flows from the south to the Mediterranean, and it is the fertile valleys of this river that sheltered one of the earliest known civilisations. The pyramids and the Sphinx, Byzantine Coptic churches and Roman ruins attract travelers from all over the world.

Egypt's population of around 64 million is generally mixed, but basically of Mediterranean stock, and the national languages are Arabic, French and English.

Every part of Africa has some green leaf that is considered a delicacy. In South Africa it is *morogo*, in Kenya *sukuma wiki*, Malawi and Zimbabwe love *ifisyasi* and *kalembula*, and Egypt's wonder is *moloukia*.

The food in Egypt is a combination of Arabic and Mediterranean, with mezes, moussaka and cannelloni forming part of the local cuisine. However, like every country, Egyptians have their authentic dishes, such as *tamia*, *foul* and *kochari*. Pigeons are also a local delicacy and, featured and gutted while you wait, they are sold in most street markets. The street café is the heart of Egyptian street life, but like much of Africa, it is a largely male preserve. They provide a pleasant atmosphere for patrons to relax over a cup of sweet Egyptian tea or Arabic coffee.

BAMIA SAUCE
Okra Sauce

SERVES 4-6

60 ml (4 T) oil
2 onions, chopped
500 g (18 oz) minced beef
500 ml (2 cups) tomato juice
1 kg (2½ lb) okra, cleaned and sliced
5 garlic cloves, crushed
3 ml (½ t) ground coriander
salt to taste

Heat 30 ml (2 T) of the oil and fry the onions until golden. Add the minced beef and brown.

Add tomato juice. Simmer for 10 minutes.

Reduce heat, add okra and stir until mixed.

In another pan, heat rest of oil and fry garlic and coriander. Add salt. Toss into okra and simmer for 7 minutes. Serve with rice or pita bread.

FETAH

SERVES 4-6

1 litre (4 cups) water
2 onions, chopped
5 cardamom seeds
salt and pepper to taste
1 kg (2½ lb) lamb, cut into cubes
6 slices white bread
15 ml (3 t) oil
10 garlic, cloves, crushed
30 ml (2 T) vinegar
500 ml (2 cups) cooked rice

In a large saucepan, bring the water to the boil and then add the onions, cardamom seeds, salt and pepper. Add the lamb and cook for about 45 minutes until tender.

Remove the meat from the broth and keep warm. Discard the cardamom seeds and mash the onion until smooth.

Cut the bread into small squares and place it in a serving dish.

Heat the oil, add the garlic and fry until pale gold. Add vinegar and boil for 3 to 5 minutes. Pour into the broth and simmer for 5 minutes.

TO SERVE: Moisten the bread with some of the broth and cover it with a thick layer of rice. Moisten the rice with the remaining soup. Arrange the meat around the rice in a ring.

KEBABS

SERVES 4-6

KOFTAS:
500 g (18 oz) minced meat
1 small onion, finely chopped
25 ml (2 T) mixed fresh herbs, such as thyme,
  basil, parsley and oregano, finely chopped
salt and pepper to taste
250 ml (1 cup) fresh breadcrumbs

500 g (18 oz) lamb cubes
2 large onions, cut into large chunks
2 firm, large tomatoes, cut into wedges

KOFTAS: Mix the minced meat, onion, herbs,
seasoning and crumbs. Form into small balls.

Thread the *koftas*, lamb cubes, onions and
tomatoes onto skewers. Grill over white-hot
charcoal until done. Serve with pita bread.

TURKEY WITH RICE AND KHALTA

SERVES 6-8

1 turkey of 1-1,5 kg (2½ - 3½ lb)
45 ml (3 T) flour
15 ml (1 T) mustard
60 ml (4 T) sugar
125 g (4½ oz)/125 ml (½ cup) butter
250 ml (1 cup) Egyptian rice
1 chicken stock cube, dissolved in 250 ml
  (1 cup) hot water
125 ml (½ cup) flaked almonds
125 ml (½ cup) each raisins and sultanas

Rub turkey with flour, leave to stand, then
rinse with water. Rub with mustard. Roast
at 180 °C (350 °F/gas 4) for 2 to 3 hours.

Melt the sugar and butter until brown. Add the
rice and stir to coat. Add the stock and heat
until boiling. Simmer until the rice is cooked.

Spoon the rice onto a platter, place the
turkey on top and sprinkle with nuts, raisins
and sultanas.

KOCHARI

SERVES 4

200 g (7 oz)/250 ml (1 cup) brown lentils
250 ml (1 cup) rice
125 ml (½ cup) macaroni
2 onions, chopped
60 ml (4 T) oil
salt and pepper to taste
1 can (410 g/14 oz) Mediterranean tomato mix

Cook the lentils, rice and macaroni separately according o the directions on the packets. Place these three ingredients together in a pot.

In another pan, fry the onions in the oil until rich brown. Remove with a slotted spoon.

Strain the oil in which the onions were fried into the lentil mixture and cook for 10 minutes, stirring lightly to prevent sticking. Season.

Serve topped with heated Mediterranean tomato mix and fried onions.

> *Kubeeba* – oval-shaped meatballs with a minced-meat filling – are served as snacks or starters. Bulgur (crushed wheat) is available from health shops, some supermarkets and delicatessens.

KUBEEBA

SERVES 4

500 g (18 oz) bulgur
500 g (18 oz) minced beef
1 onion, grated
salt and pepper to taste
oil for deep-frying

FILLING:
500 g (18 oz) minced beef
1 garlic clove, crushed
1 onion, finely chopped
pinch each of cumin, coriander and paprika
salt and pepper to taste

Soak the bulgur for 20 minutes. Drain and mix with the mince, onion and seasoning.

FILLING: Sauté the minced beef, garlic, onion, spices, salt and pepper for 20 minutes until cooked.

With wet hands, take a small piece of the bulgur-and-mince mixture and place it in the palm of your hand. With the index finger of the other hand, make a hole in the *kubeeba* and rotate, half closing the palm until it becomes very thin. Half-fill with filling and a small dot of butter. Moisten the hand again and close the *kubeeba* to form a round or egg-shaped ball.

Heat the oil and deep-fry the kubeeba on all sides until brown, or place in a greased oven tin, brush the top with cooking oil and roast in a pre-heated oven at 180 °C (350 °F/gas 4) until brown all over.

YOGHURT ZABADIE BELKHEIAR

Yoghurt with Cucumber

SERVES 4

175 ml (½ cup) natural yoghurt
1 cucumber, cut into small pieces
1 green sweet pepper, finely chopped
salt to taste

Mix all the ingredients together.

Serve as a salad.

LISAN ASFOUR
'Tongue of Bird'

SERVES 4

50 ml (¼ cup) water
250 ml (1 cup) rice pasta
500 g (18 oz) meat cubes or mince
1 onion, chopped
1 garlic clove, crushed
1 green sweet pepper, chopped
3 ml (½ t) coriander
3 ml (½ t) cumin
2 tomatoes, sliced

Heat the water to boiling point in a
saucepan. Boil the rice pasta and meat with
the onion, garlic, green pepper and spices.

Place the mixture in an oven-proof dish.
Bake in a moderate oven (180 °c/350 °F/
gas 4) for 20 minutes.

Top with the tomato slices and serve
with fried chicken.

MOLOUKIA

SERVES 4

1 bunch moloukia or spinach, finely chopped
250 ml (1 cup) chicken or meat stock
2 garlic cloves, crushed
3 ml (½ t) ground coriander
60 g (2½ oz)/62,5 ml (¼ cup) butter or
   ghee, melted

Add the moloukia to chicken or meat stock
and boil for 10 minutes.

Heat the melted butter or ghee, add
garlic and coriander and sauté. Add to the
moloukia. Serve with bread or rice and fried
chicken or meat.

UMAÍALI

SERVES 4-6

500 g (18 oz) phyllo pastry
250 ml (1 cup) mixed nuts
125 ml (½ cup) raisins
15 ml (1 T) desiccated coconut
500 ml (2 cups) milk sweetened with 62,5 ml
    (¼ cup) sugar
15 ml (1 T) butter or cream

Preheat the oven to 200 °C (400 °F/gas 6).

Bake 1 to 2 sheets of pastry at a time for
2 to 3 minutes until dry and crisp. Crush with
your fingers and place in a lightly greased
oven dish.

Mix the nuts, raisins and coconut. Scatter
this mixture on top of the crushed pastry.

Warm the sweetened milk and pour over
the dessert. Dab with butter or cream and
place in moderately hot oven until the top
is browned.

FOUL

SERVES 4-6

250 ml (1 cup) dry broad beans
250 ml (1 cup) red lentils
1 garlic clove, crushed
45 ml (3 T) oil
2 tomatoes, chopped
2 onions, chopped

Soak the beans overnight in water. Retain
the water and cook until soft.

Add the red lentils and garlic.

Heat the oil in a pan and fry the tomatoes
and onions together. Mix with the beans and
lentils. Serve hot or cold.

Kichk **is served on
its own or as part of
the mezes.**

KICHK
Milky Cold Sauce

SERVES 4

60 g (2 oz)/125 ml (½ cup) flour
salt and pepper to taste
500 ml (2 cups) tinned chicken soup
250 ml (1 cup) milk
1 onion, sliced
15 ml (1 T) butter

Mix the flour and seasoning. Add the
chicken soup to the milk and pour over the
flour, stirring to blend.

Place over a low heat and cook, stirring
constantly until slightly thickened. Place in
a shallow dish to cool.

Fry the onion in the butter until brown. Drain
and allow to cool, then place the onion over
the *kichk*. Serve cold.

VARIATION: For a green sauce, add 60 ml
(4 T) chopped fresh coriander (dhania) to the
chicken soup and milk mixture.

TAMIA

MAKES 4-6

250 ml (1 cup) chickpeas or dry beans
15 ml (1 T) chopped coriander (dhania)
15 ml (1 T) chopped dill
15 ml (1 T) chopped parsley
salt and pepper
3 ml (½ t) ground cumin
4 spring onions, chopped
pinch of bicarbonate of soda
oil for deep frying

Soak the chickpeas or beans overnight and crush.

Mix the chickpeas or dry beans with the coriander, dill and parsley. Season with salt, pepper, ground coriander and cumin.

Add spring onions and a pinch of bicarbonate of soda. Form into patties and deep-fry in hot oil. Serve with foul.

THE ABC OF AFRICAN INGREDIENTS

AGUSHI (EGUSI)
Ground melon seed, widely used in West African cooking to add a creamy texture and nutty flavour to dishes. Ground almonds can be used as a substitute.

AMADUMBE 'MADUMBIS'
A favourite of the Zulu people in Natal. These tubers have a very course, rough skin. *Amadumbes* are simply boiled in their skin until soft, peeled and then sliced or cut into wedges. They are eaten on their own as a snack or served as a side dish.

BAOBAB FRUIT
Boabab fruit is round and quite hard, and the seeds, strings and powder inside quite acidic. The powder is also used in place of cream of tartar.

BRINJAL (AUBERGINE, EGGPLANT)
An elongated or rounded fruit with a shiny purple skin. This white variety is often use in African and Mediterranean dishes.

CARDAMOM
A member of the ginger family; these seeds are also known as 'the seed of Paradise'. It is available ground or whole and is used to flavour soups, eggs, noodles, custards, breyanis, puddingsand cakes.

CASSAVA (MANDIOCA)
A tropical vegetable with tuberous roots, a brown skin and starchy flesh, similar to sweet potatoes. Cassava is commonly used in West and East African dishes. The peel is slit down to the flesh with a sharp knife, and then pulled away like a banana peel. The tuber is sliced lengthways to remove the core, which resembles thick string.

Plain boiled cassava may replace potatoes in any meal. Dried and ground, it makes cassava flour and gari.

CHILLIES
Fresh or dried chillies are widely used in African cookery. Dried, powdered chillies are known as cayenne pepper. Green chillies have more flavour and are juicier, while red chillies are hotter and must be used sparingly.

CLOVES
Zanzibar used to be the sole exporter of this precious spice. Now it is grown in a number of other countries. Cloves – the unopened buds of the *myrtaceous* tree – are picked when they turn red and are then sun dried. Ground cloves are stronger than whole ones. They are used to flavour savoury and sweet dishes.

COCONUT MILK
Widely used in East African cooking. A fresh coconut is cut or broken in half. The flesh is shredded or grated, and mixed with cold water. After a few minutes it is placed in a conical basket or colander and squeezed to produce the milk. Coconut milk can also be made by simmering desiccated coconut in water and then rubbing it through a sieve to extract the fluid.

COURGETTE (BABY MARROW, ZUCCHINI)
This vegetable, a member of the marrow family, is now used all over Africa. It has a shiny and firm watery flesh, and is best eaten when young.

COUSCOUS
The staple food in African countries such as Morocco, Tunisia and

Algeria. It is semolina that has been coarsely ground, moistened and rolled in flour.

CUMIN
An aromatic plant with long spindle-shaped seeds that are used as a condiment and a flavouring. It has a hot, piquant and slightly bitter taste.

DHANIA
Fresh coriander leaves are used to garnish curries or add flavour to savoury dishes and salads. It is also available in powdered form.

DRIED MEAT
This is especially popular in Venda and Zimbabwe. Red meat is sliced into strips and sun dried. It can be eaten on its own when dry or cooked in a ground nut sauce. In South Africa it is known as biltong; among the Shona it is known as *chumukuy*, and among the Zulus as *umqweyiba*.

FUFU
Fufu is prepared from boiled cassava (see cassava), which is prounded to a pulp and then puréed until it is free of lumps, after which it is made into balls.

GARI
Dried, ground cassava (see cassava). *Gari* can be replaced with cooked phutu.

GROUND NUTS
Ground and sifted peanuts are widely used in southern African as well as west African cooking.

GROUND NUT PASTE
This paste of ground peanuts and water is especially popular in West Africa as a ingredient of sauces and light soups. Use peanut butter as substitute.

KENKEY

This is very popular Ghanaian dish made from fermented maize-meal (see maize-meal).

MAIZE-MEAL

Ground and sometimes refined maize. Cooked to a porridge, it is a staple food of most of Africa. In Malawi it's called *nsima*, in Kenya *ugali*, and in Zimbabwe and Malawi it is called *sadza*.

MAIZE-RICE

Rice-shaped grain made from maize, popular in South African traditional cooking. It is sometimes mixed into sour porridge (*ting*).

MINT

A fresh-tasting herb with a strong flavour. In North and West Africa it is used to flavour tea.

MOPANE WORMS

Mopane worms are eaten mostly in southern Africa, and are a delicacy among the Venda, Tsonga and Pedi people. The worms fall off the mopane tree and are a rich source of protein. They are usually dried and kept for up to a year and fried in fat or cooked in a ground nut stew or tomato and onion sauce. Mopane worms are known as *mashonizha* in Venda, as *phane* in Botswana, and as *madora* or *amacimbi* in Zimbabwe.

MOROGO

Morogo is a collective term for various leaves, some of them wild. Morogo can be substituted with spinach. The different African countries have their own national green leaves, e.g. *moloukia* in Egypt, *matapa* in Malawi, *cacani* in Mozambique, *sukuma wiki* or *muchicha* in Kenya, and *rape* in Zambia and Zimbabwe.

NUTMEG

Nutmeg comes from an evergreen tree. It can be freshly grated just before using or bought ground. The dry membrane that surrounds the seed is mace.

OKRA (OKRO, THERERE)

Also referred to a ladies' fingers. Okra is widely used in African cooking. When purchasing okra, avoid the large variety, choose small firm ones.

PALM OIL

Palm oil is extracted from palm nuts which are boiled and pounded into pulp. Palm oil prepared at home is thick and red or yellowish in colour.

PEPPER

Black pepper is derived from berries that are picked just before ripening. Ripe berries are sun dried and ground to form white pepper.

PLANTAINS

Plantains are part of the banana family. Inedible when raw, but once cooked, boiled, fried, roasted or baked they have a great flavour. Used mostly in West and East Africa.

SAFFRON

A rare and expensive spice. It is used to tint and flavour savoury dished into a yellow colour. This spice is made from the stamens of the wild crocus.

SAMP

Maize kernels that have been stamped and broken but not ground as fine as maize-rice or maize-meal. It is a Xhosa staple food, but it is also eaten in most of South Africa.

SMEN (GHEE)

Smen or ghee is clarified fat, which is commonly used in North African cooking. It is also a very popular ingredient in Indian cooking. The best *smen* is made from butter.

SWEET POTATOES

These are usually reddish brown skinned, although in other parts of the continent you might find them with white skins. They can be boiled in their jacket, peeled and cooked and mashed, sliced and deep fried to make chips or oven baked.

TAMBI

Tambi is a type of egg noodle that looks like tiny ribbons. It is a favourite of Zanzibar, where it is cooked and mixed with sugar and ground cardamom.

TING

Sour or fermented porridge (Botswana).

TURMERIC (BORRIE)

Turmeric, a member of the ginger family, comes from a perennial tropical plant. The root is dried and ground and used to colour curries and rice.

WARKA

North African equivalent of phyllo pastry.

YAM

The yam is a tuber of a climbing plant. These tubers mature in the dry season and look like enormous rough potatoes. They may be egg shaped, elongated or flattened. The flesh is either yellow or white and can be eaten boiled, roasted, baked, mashed or made into chips. Sweet potatoes may be substituted for yams.

WHOLE PEPPERS

Whole peppers are used in most of Africa especially North Africa with its Mediterranean influence. These peppers can now be found in a variety of exotic colours, such as black, white and yellow. Also known as capsicums, the flavours vary according to varieties, they can be sweet, fiery, mild or hot.

INDEX